A Practical Guide

To

Obtaining Probate

Revised Edition

Peter Wade

Editor: Roger Sproston

Emerald Guides

www.straightforwardbooks.co.uk

Emerald Guides

ISBN: 978-1-80236-141-4

Printed by 4edge Ltd www.4edge.co.uk

Cover design by BW Studio Derby

CONTENTS

Introduction

INTRODUCTION

The saying goes that we can avoid everything except death and taxes. Maybe probate has the unique distinction of dealing with both these activities. We cannot avoid death but we can avoid taxes.

The proper regulation of one's estate can certainly minimise inheritance tax and maybe get rid of it entirely.

Life becomes more complicated by the day but it is possible without running up excessive legal fees to prepare a valid will and as an executor to undertake probate of someone's estate without legal help.

A good definition of probate is very high-class administration. We can do it if we follow the checklists assiduously and keep a note of everything we do. If every piece of paper is accounted for and filed properly then probate should not be too difficult. With the advent of the Internet these things are more easily undertaken by the organised amateur.

The minimum you will need is
1. Telephone
2. Computer
3. Somewhere to file all the letters.

This book attempts to take you through a typical probate transaction and to supply you with checklists, addresses, telephone numbers, and website addresses and draft letters.

I have tried to keep the text uncluttered by keeping the non-essential items to the appendixes. There will be notes in the text where these things can be found.

I purchased my first house by using a book although I did have the advantage of working in the legal department of a local authority. I knew nothing about practical conveyancing. I am a great believer in *'how to books'*. They can at the very least take out this mystique of what the professionals try to wrap up as being very complicated indeed.

Wills and probate are not brain surgery but you have to follow a procedure precisely to get it right. At the end of the process, you can save thousands in legal fees.

WRITING YOUR OWN WILL

Everyone over the age of 18 should make a will. Although in the public's view making a will is a straightforward matter it can have devastating effect if not written and executed properly and if there is no will. The safest advice is to always get a competent person to draw up and have a will executed for you. You can then rest assured that your wishes will be carried out in the event of your death.

Also, if you execute it whilst you are fit and well there is less likelihood of it being overturned by beneficiaries claiming that you were not competent to do it.

If you are in any doubt about your own ability to draw up and execute a will you should get a solicitor to do it for you. At the very least your beneficiaries will be able to sue the solicitor in the event of him or her being incompetent or your beneficiaries missing out because of negligence. If you draw up a poor will, they will regret for the rest of their lives that you had not taken competent legal advice which comes relatively cheaply for a straightforward will.

Unfortunately, the chance of inheriting does not bring out the best in people. Also, families in those circumstances do not seem to enjoy themselves more than when they are falling out over money. We all believe that it would not happen in our family as we are not so petty and mercenary but in my experience no one is exempt.

We would much rather total strangers get part of the estate than let "undeserving" members of our own family.

We all have someone to whom we do not wish to leave our estate even if it's only the taxman. Or, on intestacy, ultimately the State. If you leave it to the cats' home provided it is a charity you save the tax and keep it out of the Chancellor's hands. A satisfying outcome

WHY MAKE A WILL?

If you do not have a will then your estate will be distributed in accordance with the rules of intestacy. Intestacy means when there is no will. A testator is the maker of a will.

Apart from limited circumstances you have freedom to leave your estate to whomever you like unlike some other legal systems such as in France. You are entitled to go to the stationers and use a will form. The only problem with that is that it may work but any mistake in execution will invalidate your wishes.

Everyone should make a will and think about updating it regularly as your circumstances change. Finally, this book deals with probate in England and Wales. For information concerning Scotland: www.scotcourts.gov.uk/taking-action/dealing-with-a-deceased's-estate-in-scotland. For Northern Ireland:

www.nidirect.gov.uk/applying-probate

COVID 19 and the process of probate

It is worth mentioning the effects of the Coronavirus on the process of probate generally. As you read this book,

The Probate Registry

This is a section of HM Courts and Tribunal Services (HMCTS) that issues letters of administration or a grant of probate. Try not to worry if you haven't heard from the Probate Registry as quickly as you might have expected as HMCTS has advised that following coronavirus/COVID-19, in 2022, there may be some delays in providing grants of representation as a huge backlog has built up.

Registering the death

Registration of the death is usually done in person, however, due to the ongoing backlog in 2022, this is now usually done by telephone. The registrar will liaise with the coroner or doctor who certified the death, as well as the funeral director, to minimise face-to-face contact. The death certificate can then be applied for online and sent to you or your professional advisor.

Administering an estate

Simple estates

We discuss administration of estates further on in the book. In brief, if the estate is simple, for example, everything is jointly owned or the estate is valued at less than £5,000, you may not need a grant of representation and you should be able to administer the estate without professional help.

More complex estates

If the estate is more complex, you are likely to need the assistance of a professional.

This might include estates where:

- There are a variety of assets, including property that needs to be sold
- There is a possibility that the will might be disputed, for example where a dependant has been left out and it is likely that they will want to make a claim
- Some assets are held in trusts, or there is a request in the will that a trust is set up
- There are missing beneficiaries
- The value of the estate is substantial and may exceed the inheritance tax threshold

If multiple properties, overseas property, investments or businesses are included in the estate or inheritance tax issues are likely, professional help will be required.

In chapter 1, we discuss probate generally.

****

Chapter 1

Probate Generally

What is probate?

When a person dies, it is necessary for someone to be appointed, with legal authority, to manage the deceased's financial affairs and wind up his/her estate. In law, the uncompleted financial matters of a deceased are known as 'the estate' and the person who is given the legal authority to wind up the estate is called the legal personal representative. After the application for probate, the document which proves the legal authority of the personal representative is called the grant of representation to an estate.

Where to get a grant of representation to an estate

Grants of representation to an estate are obtained from an office of the High Court known as the Probate Registry. The process of obtaining the grant is commonly known as 'probate'.

If someone leaves a will but dies without appointing an executor to carry out the terms of that will, or if the executors who are appointed by the will are unable or unwilling to carry out the duties of an executor, then the grant of representation obtained from the probate registry to prove that the will is a valid one and to authorize the person who obtains it to carry out its terms is called 'letters of administration with the will annexed'. If someone dies without making a will, that person dies intestate and the grant of representation obtained from the probate registry to authorize someone to wind up the estate is called 'letters of administration of the estate'. Those who obtain letters of administration are known as administrators of the estate. The main difference between the executor appointed under the will and the administrator of an estate are that an executor's powers are given by the will and are more or less immediate whereas the administrators powers cannot be exercised until the Registry has appointed the administrator.

Presumption of Death Act 2013

The Presumption of Death Act, 2013 allows relatives to apply for a single certificate declaring someone presumed dead, helping them resolve that person's affairs.

Its creation follows a campaign by the charity Missing People, and relatives of missing people, including Peter Lawrence, father of missing chef Claudia Lawrence, and Rachel Elias, the sister of Manic Street Preachers guitarist Richey Edwards who went missing in 1995. Their concerns were raised before the Justice Select Committee and the All-Party Parliamentary Group for Runaway and Missing Children and Adults, and the new law was passed.

The law, based on the Scottish Presumption of Death Act 1977, only allows families to apply for a presumption of death order after seven years.

Essentially, probate and letters of administration can be seen as title documents to the assets of the deceased person's estate. However, there are a few assets where they are not required and can be dispensed with. These include what are known as nominated assets, jointly owned assets owned as joint tenants, estates of small value and estates which consist entirely of personal effects and/or personal currency. There may however still be a requirement to deal with HMRC in relation to inheritance tax.

If in doubt contact the HMRC helpline 0300 123 1072 and outside UK 44+ 300 123 1072.

Property held jointly

Assets owned jointly are those that are not held in the sole name of the deceased. In English law, there are two ways of owning property jointly, either as joint tenants or tenants in common. In this sense, the word tenant doesn't mean tenant in the sense of landlord and tenant but is used universally in relationship to ownership of property.

If property is held as joint tenants the law clearly states that on the death of one of the owners, that person's share of the property does not become part of his estate (except for the purposes of Inheritance tax), it is inherited by the surviving joint owners, regardless of what is contained within the will. However, if property is held as tenants in common, the law states that on the death of one owner that persons share of the jointly owned property does become part of his or her estate.

The line between jointly owned property and property held as tenants in common is fine. However, there are a few obvious indicators. Usually, if bank or building society accounts are held jointly, along with stock and shares, they are considered joint tenancies. However, there must be evidence of equal ownership of property.

Any evidence to the contrary such as unequal payments, or sharing of rents, dividends etc, can mean tenancy in common.

Value of the estate-Estates valued under £15,000 gross
If the value of an estate before deducting the cost of the funeral and any debts left by the deceased is under £15,000, it is usually worth contacting organizations such as banks or building societies holding assets, to request that they make payment to the personal representative without going through the formalities of obtaining a grant of representation. They may or may not co-operate but it is worth contacting them. If the amounts involved are low then banks or building societies will co-operate on sight of a valid original will or if there is no will, they will deal with the next of kin and a solicitor.

Obtaining a grant of representation and letters of administration
There are a number of main steps involved in obtaining probate or letters of administration with the will annexed or letters of administration and then administering the estate shown overleaf:

- Obtaining the information necessary to fill out the paperwork to obtain the grant of representation.
- preparing the documentation and then lodging the documentation to obtain an inheritance tax assessment and the issue of the grant of representation.
- Registering the grant in connection with the various assets and giving instructions as to how they are to be dealt with and collecting what is due to the estate.

Following the completion of the three main steps above there are a further three steps:
- Finalise the income and Capital gains tax positions
- Pay off the debts and discharge the liabilities of the estate.
- Distribute the remaining assets of the estate to the beneficiaries.

Dealing with the estate yourself or employing a solicitor

There are obvious advantages to using a solicitor. These are that solicitors are trained in law and can usually give sound guidance. They are usually necessary when it comes to complicated wills. They will take a lot of the work away from the executor which can be very helpful. They also have insurance to cover themselves against negligence. The obvious disadvantages can be the cost. Solicitors charge anything from between £150-250 per hour. In addition, a percentage charge can be made depending on the value of the estate. This is usually between 1-2% of the estate depending on value. If you intend to use a solicitor, make sure you are fully acquainted with the costs before you instruct them to act.

Problems with personal representatives

In some cases, a will can specify an executor but that person is unwilling to act. Generally speaking, there is no legal obligation upon an executor or any other person entitled to apply for a grant of representation to apply for one. A person can give up their right to apply by signing a document to that effect, but this document is not binding until it is lodged with a probate registry.

When it has been lodged with a Registry, he or she cannot then change their mind unless permitted by the court, which is rare. The only person who cannot refuse to take out a grant of representation is an executor of a will who has 'intermeddled' with an estate, which means someone who has already done something which shows an intention to act as executor or apply for a grant of probate.

Removing someone unsuitable to act

If a person who has already taken out a grant of representation to an estate behaves in a manner which is considered improper in relation to the estate or proves unsuitable in some other way, it is then usually possible to commence proceedings in a court to ask that he or she be removed from the position of personal representative and someone else replace him or her.

Stopping an application for a grant

If someone who is claiming an interest in an estate feels that an application has been made which should not be issued and he or she wants to make their views known to the registry, he or she can give notice to the registry that they wish to be heard before a grant is made. This notice, which is called a caveat, must be in writing and signed by the person issuing the notice.

This caveat will last for six months and while it is in force no grant of representation, other than one limited to those below can be made:

- the administration of an estate until the conclusion of litigation currently taking place in the Chancery Division of the High Court in relation to the estate
- the preservation of an estate which will be endangered by delays in administering it.

****

Chapter 2

Drafting A Practical Will-Taking all Matters into Account

Creating a clear and unambiguous will can greatly assist the process of probate in the future.

Revocation of Wills

Once having drafted a will you might want to change it. There are several ways to go about revoking your will. The best way is to draft a new will and state you are revoking all prior wills. If you don't want to draft a new will, then you can revoke a will by executing a codicil. You can also revoke a will by physically destroying it, but this method carries risks. There are statutory rules as to revocation of wills, the most important ones being marriage and divorce. There are other matters to be aware of, one of the most important being inheritance tax.

Inheritance tax

Inheritance Tax is a tax on the estate (the property, money and possessions) of someone who's died. There's normally no Inheritance Tax to pay if either:

- the value of the estate is below the £325,000 threshold
- a person leaves everything to their spouse or civil partner, a charity, or a community amateur sports club

If the estate's value is below the threshold a person will still need to report it to HMRC. If a person gives away their home to their children (including adopted, foster or stepchildren) or grandchildren the threshold can increase to £500,000 (2022/2023).

If a person is married or in a civil partnership and their estate is worth less than the threshold, any unused threshold can be added to their partner's threshold when they die. This means their threshold can be as much as £900,000.

Inheritance Tax rates

The standard Inheritance Tax rate is 40%. It's only charged on the part of the estate that's above the threshold.

Example An estate is worth £500,000 and the tax-free threshold is £325,000. The Inheritance Tax charged will be 40% of £175,000 (£500,000 minus £325,000). The estate can pay Inheritance Tax at a reduced rate of 36% on some assets if a person leaves 10% or more of the 'net value' to charity in their will. For a very good guide to inheritance tax go to: www.moneyadviceservice.org.uk/en/articles/a-guide-to-inheritance-tax

Reliefs and exemptions

Some gifts given while alive may be taxed after death. Depending on when a person gave the gift, 'taper relief' might mean the Inheritance Tax charged is less than 40%.

Other reliefs, such as Business Relief, allow some assets to be passed on free of Inheritance Tax or with a reduced bill.

A person should contact the Inheritance Tax and probate helpline on 0300 123 1072 about Agricultural Relief if their estate includes a farm or woodland.

Passing on a home

A person can pass a home to their husband, wife, or civil partner when they die. There's no Inheritance Tax to pay if they do this.

If a person leaves the home to another person in their will, it counts towards the value of the estate.

If a person owns their home (or a share in it) their tax-free threshold can increase to £500,000 if:

- they leave it to their children (including adopted, foster or stepchildren) or grandchildren
- the estate is worth less than £2 million

Giving away a home before a person dies

There's normally no Inheritance Tax to pay if a person moves out and lives for another 7 years. If a person wants to continue living in their property after giving it away, they will need to:

- pay rent to the new owner at the going rate (for similar local rental properties)
- pay their share of the bills
- live there for at least 7 years

They do not have to pay rent to the new owners if both the following apply:

- they only give away part of your property
- the new owners also live at the property

If a person dies within 7 years

If a person dies within 7 years of giving away all or part of their property, their home will be treated as a gift and the 7-year rule applies.

Gifts

There's usually no Inheritance Tax to pay on small gifts a person makes out of their normal income, such as Christmas or birthday presents. These are known as 'exempted gifts'.

There's also no Inheritance Tax to pay on gifts between spouses or civil partners. A person can give them as much as they like during their lifetime, as long as they live in the UK permanently.

Other gifts count towards the value of the estate.

People that a person gives gifts to will be charged Inheritance Tax if they give away more than £325,000 in the 7 years before their death.

What counts as a gift

A gift can be:
- anything that has a value, such as money, property, possessions

- a loss in value when something's transferred, for example if a person sells their house to their child for less than it's worth, the difference in value counts as a gift

Exempted gifts

A person can give away £3,000 worth of gifts each tax year (6 April to 5 April) without them being added to the value of the estate. This is known as the 'annual exemption'. A person can carry any unused annual exemption forward to the next year - but only for one year. Each tax year, they can also give away:

- wedding or civil ceremony gifts of up to £1,000 per person (£2,500 for a grandchild or great-grandchild, £5,000 for a child)
- normal gifts out of income, for example Christmas or birthday presents - they must be able to maintain their standard of living after making the gift
- payments to help with another person's living costs, such as an elderly relative or a child under 18
- gifts to charities and political parties

A person can use more than one of these exemptions on the same person - for example, they could give your grandchild gifts for her birthday and wedding in the same tax year.

Small gifts up to £250

A person can give as many gifts of up to £250 per person as they want during the tax year as long as they have not used another exemption on the same person.

The 7-year rule

If there's Inheritance Tax to pay, it's charged at 40% on gifts given in the 3 years before a person dies. Gifts made 3 to 7 years before death are taxed on a sliding scale known as 'taper relief'.

Years between gift and death	Tax paid
less than 3	40%
3-4	32%
4-5	24%
5-6	16%
6-7	8%
7 or more	0%

Gifts are not counted towards the value of the estate after 7 years.

When someone living outside the UK dies

If their permanent home ('domicile') is abroad, Inheritance Tax is only paid on their UK assets, for example property or bank accounts they have in the UK. It's not paid on 'excluded assets' like:

- foreign currency accounts with a bank or the Post Office
- overseas pensions
- holdings in authorised unit trusts and open-ended investment companies

There are different rules if a person has assets in a trust or government gilts, or they are a member of visiting armed forces.

When you will not count as living abroad

HMRC will treat a person as being domiciled in the UK if they either:

- lived in the UK for 15 of the last 20 years
- had their permanent home in the UK at any time in the last 3 years of their life

Double-taxation treaties

An executor might be able to reclaim tax through a double-taxation treaty if Inheritance Tax is charged on the same assets by the UK and the country where a person lived.

Post Death Planning
DEED OF VARIATION

Within the two-year period after the death the will can effectively be rewritten to take advantage of the nil-rate Inheritance Tax band. This is made by Deed of Family arrangement. All the beneficiaries must agree to this.

Sample Will-recommended layout and clauses

COMMENCEMENT: Name and address of Testator

This is the last will and testament of me ^^^^^^^ of ^^^^^^^ in the County of ^^^^^-

Formal revocation of all previous wills

I REVOKE all former Wills and Testamentary dispositions made by me-Funeral arrangements

I WISH that my body be buried/cremated-

Appointment of sole executor who is usually wife/ husband who is also sole beneficiary

I APPOINT my ^^^^ to be my sole Executor/Executrix and I GIVE AND BEQUEATH to ^^^^^ all my property both real and personal whatsoever and wheresoever absolutely PROVIDED that ^^^^^^ survives me by at least thirty days but if my said ^^^^ shall not so survive me I DIRECT that the remaining clauses hereof shall take effect-

Appointment of executor and alternative executor if first one predeceases

 (1) I APPOINT my ^^^^ ("my ^^^^) to be the sole executor ^^^ of this Will but if that appointment fails (because ^^^^ dies before me or before proving the Will or is unable or unwilling to act or for any other reason) I APPOINT ^^^^^ of ^^^^^^ and ^^^^^^ of ^^^^^ to be the executors and trustees of the Will-

IN THIS WILL and any Codicil to it the expression "my Trustees" means its trustees for the time being or (where the context requires) my personal representatives for the time being-

ANY POWERS given to the trustees of this Will (by the Will or any Codicil to it or by the general law) may be exercised by my Trustees before the administration of my estate is complete and even before a grant or representation has been obtained-

Appointment of professional firm to be executors
NB charging clause

(1) I APPOINT the partners at the date of my death in the firm of ^^^^^^^^^^^^ of ^^^^^^^^^^^^^^ or the firm which at that date has succeeded to and carries on its practice and I EXPRESS the wish that one and only one of those partners (or if the appointment of ^^^^ fails for any reason to take effect then two and only two of them) shall prove the Will and act initially it its trusts-

(2) IN THIS WILL the expression "my Trustees" means my Executors and Trustees of this Will and of any trust arising under it-

(3) ANY POWERS given to the trustees of this Will (by the Will or any Codicil to it or by the general law) my be exercised by my Trustees before the administration of my estate is complete and even before a grant or representation has been obtained-

Appointment of solicitors

(1) I APPOINT as my Executors and Trustees ^^ and the partners at the date of my death in the firm of ^^^^^^^^^ of ^^^^^^^^^^ or the firm which at that date has succeeded to and carries on its practice and I EXPRESS the wish that one and only one of those partners (or if the appointment of ^^^^ fails for any reason to take effect then two and only two of them) shall prove the Will and act initially in its trusts-

(2) IN THIS WILL the expression "my Trustees" means my Executors and Trustees of this Will and of any trust arising under it-

(3) ANY POWERS given to the trustees of this Will by the Will or any Codicil to it or by the general law) may be exercised by my Trustees before the administration of my estate is complete and even before a grant or representation has been obtained-

NORMAL APPOINTMENT OF EXECUTORS

(1) I APPOINT ^^^^^^ and ^^^^^ to be the Executors and Trustees of this my Will (hereinafter called "my Trustees)-

(2) IN THIS WILL the expression "my Trustees" means my Executors and Trustees of this Will and of any trust arising under it-

(3) ANY POWERS given to the Trustees of this Will (by the Will or any Codicil to it or by the general law) may be exercised by my Trustees before the administration of my estate is complete and even before a grant has been obtained-

I APPOINT ^^^^^ and his wife ^^^^^ and the survivor of them of ^^^^^^ and any person or persons appointed by him/her/them to act after his/her/their death or incapacity to be the guardians during minority of any children of mine who are the minors at the date of death of the survivor of me and my ^^^^^^-

Specific Legacies including personal chattels I GIVE AND BEQUEATH all my personal chattels as defined by Section 55(1)

(x) of the Administration of Estates Act 1925 unto ^^^^^ absolutely-

I GIVE AND BEQUEATH all my personal chattels as defined by Section 55(1)(x) of the Administration of Estates Act 1925 unto my Trustees Upon Trust to dispose of the same as they in their absolute discretion shall think fit or in accordance with any note or memorandum which may be found amongst my papers at my death-

I GIVE AND BEQUEATH to ^^^^^ such of my personal chattels (as the same are defined by Section 55(1) (x) of the Administration of Estates Act 1925) as ^^^^^ may within two months of the date of my death select and I GIVE AND BEQUEATH all personal chattels remaining after ^^^^ has made ^^^^^ selection or the period for making such selection has expired to ^^^^-

Pecuniary legacies

I GIVE AND BEQUEATH the following specific legacies free of Inheritance Tax other fiscal impositions and of costs of transfer-

(1) ^^^^^^

(2) ^^^^^^

I GIVE AND BEQUEATH the following pecuniary legacies free of Inheritance Tax and other fiscal impositions: -

(1) To ^^^^^^^^ the sum of ^^^^^

(2) To ^^^^^^^^ the sum of ^^^^^

Pecuniary legacies to charities etc

I DECLARE that the receipt of the treasurer or other proper officer for the time being of ^^^^^ shall be a sufficient discharge to my Trustees for any legacy hereby given- *(Not necessary if using STEP provisions)*

 (1) WITH REFERENCE to Section 31 of the trustee Act 1925 the words "may in all circumstances be reasonable" shall be omitted from paragraph 1 of subsection 1 and in substitution therefore the words "the Trustees may think fit" shall be inserted and the proviso at the end of subsection 1 shall be omitted-

(2) With reference to Section 32 of the Trustee Act 1925 provision A of subsection 1 shall be deemed to be omitted-

RECEIPT FROM CHARITY

THE RECEIPT of anyone purporting to be the treasurer or other proper officer of any charitable or other body to which any gift is made by (or under any provision of) this Will or any Codicil to it shall be a good discharge to my Trustees for the gift- *(Not necessary if STEP provisions being used)*

UNDERAGE BENEFICIARY

IF any legatee hereunder (whether specific or pecuniary) shall be a minor at my death my Trustees may if they think fit pay transfer or deliver the legacy to such legatee personally or to his parent or guardian and the receipt of such legatee notwithstanding his minority or of such parent or guardian shall be a sufficient discharge to my Trustees for such legacy who shall not be further concerned as to the application thereof-

Residuary estate

I GIVE DEVISE AND BEQUEATH all my real and the residue of my personal property whatsoever and wheresoever not hereinbefore specifically disposed of unto my Trustees upon trust to sell call in and convert the same into money with power to postpone the sale calling in and conversion thereof for so long as they in their absolute discretion shall think fit without being liable for loss-

I GIVE DEVISE AND BEQUEATH all my property both real and personal whatsoever and wheresoever unto my Trustees upon trust to sell call in and convert the same into money with power to postpone the sale calling in and conversion thereof for so long as they in their absolute discretion shall think fit without being liable for loss-

Duties of executors

MY TRUSTEES shall stand possessed of the net proceeds of such sale calling in and conversion as aforesaid and my ready money upon trust to pay thereout my debts funeral and testamentary expenses and all duty and taxes payable by reason of my death and after such payment in trust for my said ^^^^^^ absolutely and if ^^^^^^ shall predecease me then in trust for such of my children as shall survive me and attain the age of ^^^^ years and if more than one in equal shares absolutely-

PER STIRPES - Grandchildren taking the share their parent would have received if they had lived.

PROVIDED always that if any of my said children shall predecease me leaving issue living at my death who shall attain the age of ^^^ years such issue shall take by substitution per stirpes and if more then one in equal shares the share of my estate which his hers or their parent would have taken had he or she survived me-

RESIDUARY ESTATE

I GIVE all my property not otherwise disposed of by this my Will unto my Trustees upon trust to sell the same (with power to postpone sale) and out of the moneys to arise from such sale to pay my debts legacies my funeral and testamentary expenses and all duty and taxes payable by reason of my death and TO HOLD the residue of the said proceeds of sale in trust for ^^^^^ for ^^^^^ own use and benefit absolutely-

I GIVE all the residue of my estate (out of which shall be paid my funeral and testamentary expenses and my debts) and any property over which I have at my death any general power of appointment to my Trustees ON TRUST to sell call in and convert into money but with full power to postpone doing so for as long as they see fit without being liable for loss (and such estate and property and the property which currently represents it is referred to in this Will as "the Trust Fund")-

MY TRUSTEES shall hold the Trust Fund ON TRUST: -

(1)   To pay its income to my said wife/husband for his/her life (but contingently on surviving me for twenty-eight days) and

(2) without becoming entitled to the income during that period except in that event) and subject to that:-

(3) Absolutely for such of my children as are alive at the death of the survivor of my said wife/husband and me and reach the age of ^^^ years and if more than one in equal shares PROVIDED that if any child of mine dies (in my lifetime or after my death) before attaining a vested interest but leaves a child or children alive at the death of the survivor of my said wife/husband my child and me who reach the age of ^^^^ years then such child or children shall take absolutely and if more than one in equal shares so much of the Trust Fund as that child of mine would have taken on attaining a vested interest-

I GIVE DEVISE AND BEQUEATH all the residue of my property both real and personal whatsoever and wheresoever not otherwise disposed of by this my Will and any Codicil hereto unto my Trustees upon trust for sale (with power to postpone such sale) to pay my debts funeral and testamentary expenses pecuniary legacies and all duties and other taxes payable by reason my death and to hold the net proceeds of sale upon trust for such of my children who survive me and attain the age of ^^^^ years and if more than one in equal shares absolutely PROVIDED ALWAYS that if any such child of mine shall die in my lifetime leaving issue who survive me and attain the age of ^^^ years then such issue shall take by substitution and more than one in equal shares per stirpes the share of my residuary estate which such deceased child of mine would have taken had he or she survived me and attained a vested interest under this my Will-

IF the foregoing provisions shall fail then my Trustees shall hold my residuary estate for ^^^^ and ^^^^ or the survivor or survivors of them in equal shares absolutely-

FAILURE OF GIFT / SHARE AND THE BALANCE TO GO TO RESIDUARY ESTATE

IF the trusts hereinbefore declared of and concerning any share of my residuary estate shall fail or determine then from the date of such failure or determination such shares shall accrue and be added to the other shares of my residuary estate in equal proportions and be held upon the like trusts and subject to the like powers and provisions as those affecting such other shares-

SURVIVORSHIP CLAUSE

EVERY person who would otherwise benefit under this Will but who fails to survive me for thirty days shall be deemed to have predeceased me for the purpose of ascertaining the devolution of my estate and the income from my estate during the period of thirty days from my death shall be accumulated and added to capital accordingly-

IN this Will or any Codicil to it the Standard provisions of the Society of Trust and Estate Practitioners (First Edition) shall apply-

Extension of executor's powers

MY TRUSTEES may in extension of the power of appropriation conferred on personal representatives by Section 41 of the Administration of Estates Act 1925 at any time at their discretion appropriate any part of my estate in its then actual condition or state of investments in or towards satisfaction of any legacy or any share in my estate without the necessity of obtain the consent of any person- *(Not necessary if STEP provisions are used)*

IN ADDITION to all other powers conferred by law my Trustees may at any time and from time to time raise the whole or any part of the vested contingent expectant or presumptive share or shares of any beneficiary hereunder and pay the same to or apply the same for the advancement maintenance education or otherwise howsoever for the benefit of such beneficiary-

ANY MONEYS requiring investment hereunder may be laid out in or upon the acquisition or security of any property of whatsoever nature and wheresoever situate to the intent that my Trustees shall have the same full and unrestricted power of investing in all respects as if they were absolutely entitled thereto beneficially- *(Not necessary if STEP provisions are used)*

POWER TO INSURE

MY TRUSTEES may insure any trust property (including property to which someone is absolutely entitled) for any amount (including an amount which allows for increases in costs and expenses through inflation or otherwise) against any risks (including the risk of any kind of consequential loss and the risk of public or third part liability) and may pay the premiums out of the income or the capital of the property insured or any other property held on the same trust-*(Not necessary if STEP provisions are used)*

I DECLARE that all income received after my death shall be treated and applied as income from whatever source or class of investment or property the same shall arise and even if the property in respect of which the income arises is sold for the payment of my debts or for other purposes and whatever the period may be in respect of which the income shall have accrued and that no property not actually producing income shall be treated as producing income-

CHARGING CLAUSE FOR PROFESSIONAL EXECUTORS

ANY TRUSTEE being a person engaged in a profession or business may act and be paid for all work done and time expended by himself or his firm in like manner as if he not having been appointed a Trustee hereof had been employed by the Trustees to do such work including acts of business which a Trustee not being engaged in such profession or business could have done personally-*(Not necessary if STEP provisions are used)*

Attestation clause

IN WITNESS whereof I have hereunto set my hand this   day of   Two Thousand ^^^^

SIGNED by the said ^^^^^^ the Testator/Testatrix as and for his/her last Will and testament in the presence of us both being present at the same time who at his/her request in his/her presence and in the presence of each other have hereunto subscribed our name as witnesses-

SIGNED by the above named ^^^^^^ in our joint presence and then by us in his-

SIGNED by the above named ^^^^ in our joint presence and then by us in hers-

SIGNED by the said ^^^^^ the Testatrix and as for her last Will and testament in the presence of us both present at the same time who at her request in her presence and in the presence of each other have hereunto subscribed our names as witnesses-

CODICILS

For Codicils.......

IN all other respects I confirm my said Will

IN WITNESS whereof I have hereunto set my hand this day of Two Thousand and ^^^^^^

SIGNED by the said ^^^^^^^^^^^^^^^^^^^^^^^^^^^^^^^^)

As a Codicil to her Will in the joint presence of us both)
Present at the same time who at her request in her)
presence and in the presence of each other have)
hereunto subscribed our names as witnesses-)

TRUSTS

This is an area of law which can confuse the person in the street as it is a term that is used but not fully understood. It is in effect a legal device by which assets may be held on behalf of another.

The most basic trust is when a person under 18 who cannot give a valid receipt has assets held on his or her behalf until they reach the age of majority. Before the age of 18 the assets will be held by trustees and during that time the assets will be held on trust.

TRUSTEES

These are the people who have control of the property and take responsibility for the running of the trust.

BENEFICIARIES

These are the people who have the benefit of the trusts

WHY A TRUST SHOULD BE CREATED

➢ They are used for a variety of purposes
➢ To preserve assets which people retain in the family from being dissipated.
➢ As previously mentioned for land and other property to be held on behalf of a child who is incapable of holding such property in their own right. This arises because a minor cannot give a valid receipt for property.
➢ To create a pension fund
➢ To operate investments on behalf of others such as unit trusts
➢ As a tax saving device.

The situations where a trust might arise are as follows:

Children

If you wish to make a gift to a child then a trust is necessary for legal reasons.

LIFE INTERESTS

If the testator wishes to leave property to another to be held by them during their lifetime and thereafter to another. This would arise if say on a second marriage the testator wanted to allow his wife to reside in the matrimonial home and once she died the property to go to his children. The wife would be what is known as the life tenant and has the right to occupy the property during her lifetime. The wife therefore merely has the life interest and the property is held on trust for both her and the children

CONTINGENT INTERESTS

This is when a gift is given on a condition or contingent basis. The most common example is when a gift is made to someone until they achieve a certain age such as 21 or 25. If a gift is given immediately is known as vested. When there is a condition, it is contingent that is awaiting the passing of some event on this occasion the age of 21 or 25.

DIFFERENT TYPES OF TRUSTS

THE DISCRETIONARY TRUST

This can be used for tax planning purposes. It gives the trustees the right that is the discretion to deal with the property in the trust as they see fit.

THE ACCUMULATION AND MAINTENANCE TRUST

These are used for the benefit of children and grandchildren

THE INTEREST IN POSSESSION TRUST

This is where the beneficiaries have the right to use the property.

WHAT CAN THE TRUSTEES DO?

The trustees' powers come from a variety of sources being from the trust deed itself, Statutory authority, and common law authority.

****

Chapter 3

Being Aware of Lasting Powers of Attorney and Enduring Powers of Attorney

---

Lasting Powers of Attorney

Lasting Power of Attorney is a legal document which gives authority to another person to make decisions on your behalf. This is obviously someone you can trust to make decisions on your behalf. The Attorney you choose will be able to make decisions for you when you become lacking in mental capacity or simply no longer wish to do so. There are two types of Lasting Power of Attorney. There is:

- Property and Financial Lasting Power of Attorney, which allows your attorney to deal with your property and finances.
- Health and Welfare which allows your attorney to make care decisions on your behalf when you lack mental capacity to do so.

A Lasting Power of Attorney cannot be used until it is registered with the Office of the Public Guardian. By having a Lasting Power of Attorney you are ensuring a safe way of having decisions made for you. The following reasons for this are:

- It must be registered with the Office of the Public Guardian before it can be used

- You can choose someone to provide a 'certificate', which means they confirm that you understand the significance and purpose of what you're agreeing to. This is normally a solicitor or legal expert
- You can choose who gets told about your Lasting Power of Attorney when it is registered (so they have an opportunity to raise concerns). This may be a relative or someone close to you
- Your signature and the signatures of your chosen attorneys must be witnessed
- Your attorney(s) must follow the Code of Practice of the Mental Capacity Act 2005 and act in your best interests
- The Office of the Public Guardian provides helpful support and advice

The Mental Capacity Act 2005

The Attorney's must follow the code of the Mental Capacity Act 2005. Copies of this can be obtained from direct.gov.uk/mental capacity.

The main principles of the Act are:
- They must assume that you can make your own decisions
- They must help you to make as many decisions as you can

Your Attorney's must make decisions and act in your best interests when you are unable to make the decisions yourself.

What is Mental Capacity?

In everyday life we make decisions about various matters in our lives. We call this ability to make these decision 'Mental Capacity'. Some people may experience some difficulty in making decisions and this may be due to various reasons such as, a mental health problem, a learning disability or have had a stroke or brain injury. The Mental Capacity Act of 2005 has more guidance on how to assess someone's ability to make decisions

This act covers decisions in areas such as property and financial affairs and health and welfare etc. It also covers everyday decisions such as personal care. The Act also sets out five principles that are the basis of the legal requirement of the Act.

Unless it can be proved otherwise, every adult has the right to make their own decisions. All available help must be given before they are deemed not to be able to make their own decisions. Any decision made for a person who is unable to so for themselves must be done in their best interests. Any decisions made for someone else should not restrict their basic rights and freedoms.

The Court of Protection has the power to make decisions about whether someone lacks mental capacity. It can also appoint deputies to act and make decisions on behalf of someone who is unable to do so on their own.

Enduring Powers of Attorney (EPA's)

No more Enduring Powers of Attorney may be created after the

1st of October 2008, but there are Enduring Powers of Attorney which are in existence and they are perfectly legally valid.

It is a legal document by which the Donor give the legal right to one or more Attorney's to manage the Donor's property and financial affairs.

The document allows the Attorney's to do anything that the Donor would have been able to do for themselves.

General Powers of Attorney

A General Power of Attorney can still be created but this ends when the Donor lacks mental capacity, but an Enduring Power of Attorney continues even once this capacity no longer exists.

Under an enduring Power of Attorney, once the Donor becomes mentally incapable the Attorney will need to apply to Register the Enduring Power of Attorney with the OPG. Enduring Powers of Attorney were created under the Enduring Powers of Attorney Act 1985 which has been repealed by the Mental Capacity Act of 2005. The capacity to create an EPA was assumed to exist unless it was proven to the contrary. If a person has mental capacity, then Enduring Power of Attorney can be used like an Ordinary Power of Attorney. Once the mental capacity has lost this has to be registered.

Under an Enduring Power of Attorney, Attorney's may be appointed jointly or jointly and severally. Whereas with a single Attorney, that Attorney should sign on each occasion where two or more Attorneys are appointed, they can be joint or joint and several. Jointly means both Attorney's need to sign on every occasion. Joint and Several means that either of the Attorneys could both sign but are not required to sign on each occasion. Both are not required to sign on each occasion.

Registration of an EPA

When an Attorney has reason to believe that the Donor has become mentally incapable he must apply to register the EPA. Registration is made by completing the prescribed forms and giving notice to certain individuals who are entitled to receive notice of the intended registration.

Various parties are entitled to receive notice of intention to register and notice should be sent to:

- The Donor
- The Attorney's
- Close relatives of the Donor

There is a list of relatives to whom the notice should be given. Once up to three close relatives have been notified the provisions have been complied with.

The Difference Between Enduring Powers of Attorney and Lasting Powers of Attorney

As stated, there cannot now be created an Enduring Power of Attorney, since the 30th of September 2007. With a Lasting Power of Attorney, it must contain names or persons who the donor wishes to be notified of any application and must contain the

Certificate that the donor understands the purpose of the instrument.

Decisions made under an LPA/EPA
Under an EPA the attorneys can do anything with the Donor's property and financial affairs but cannot make decisions about the Donor's personal welfare. Under an LPA the Attorney's can make decisions about property and financial affairs and personal welfare, including refusing consent to treatment. The latter applies only if the Donor lacks, or that the Attorney reasonably believes that the Donor lacks mental capacity.

Who Can Create a Lasting Power of Attorney?
Anyone can create a Lasting Power of Attorney and it can also be described as the Capacity, that is those who are able make a Lasting Power of Attorney. The Donor (the person making the LPA) must be at least 18 years of age and must have the mental capacity to execute under the Mental Health Act 2005.

The definition of lack of capacity is if a person lacks capacity in relation to a matter if at the material time, he is unable to make a decision for himself in relation to the matter because of an impairment or of a disturbance in the functioning of the mind or brain. This may be either a temporary or permanent disturbance.

There is a presumption that a person can be assumed to have mental capacity unless it is established that he lacks capacity. All people over the age of 18 years of age are presumed to be capable of making their own decisions. The standard of proof is on a balance of probabilities. The Lasting Power of Attorney includes a certificate by a person of a prescribed description that at the time the Donor executes the instrument that:

- The Donor understood the purpose of the instrument and the scope of the authority conferred under it.
- No fraud or undue pressure is used to induce the Donor to create an LPA
- There is nothing else which would prevent an LPA from being created from the instrument.

The current Fees for Registering a Power of Attorney can be found on:

www.gov.uk/enduring-power-attorney-duties/register-an-enduring-power-of-attorney.

The Lasting Power of Attorney can be cancelled at any time as long as the person giving it has mental capacity to cancel

What happens if there is no LPA?
If there is no LPA, then an application will need to be made to the Court of Protection at considerably more cost and with no guarantee that the right person will be appointed as the Deputy as it is named.

Creating a Lasting Power of Attorney

The forms can be found on the Ministry of Justice website. The Registration must be done correctly and if there is a defect in the form may result in the refusal of the registration. Once the LPA has been signed errors cannot be simply corrected although the OPG may allow certain amendments.

Executing the LPA – it must be signed by the Donor, the Certificate provider and the Attorneys in the correct order.

Execution by the Donor or the Attorneys must take place in the presence of a witness.

Restrictions on who can act as a witness are:

- The Donor and the Attorney must not witness each other's signature.

It is also suggested that neither the Donor's spouse or civil partner witness the LPA.

****

Chapter 4

Before the Grant of Probate-Estate Valuation and General Tasks

---

When a person dies and the process of obtaining probate begins, there are certain matters such as the registration of death and estate valuation, which you will need to be aware of.

Administration of the estate

This is a general term relating to the winding up of the estate. It must be done whether there is a will and executors are appointed or if there is no will and an administrator takes over the duties of the winding up the estate. The estate is of course all the assets and liabilities of the deceased. The public tends to think of an estate as meaning only freehold land as in a landed estate. Lawyers of course mean all the deceased's worldly goods, whether freehold leasehold or personal.

Immediate steps

Registration of the death

Normally the lawyers will not be involved in the registration of the death but if you do any amount of probate, you will be called upon to do it because there are no close relatives or the firm are the executors. The responsibility of registering the death is usually upon a relative but any person present may undertake it. When the solicitor is the executor then he/ she can discharge the duty. It must be registered in the district where the death took place or the body was found.

The death should be registered within five days but an extension can be granted. The registrar will liaise with the coroner or doctor who certified the death, as well as the funeral director, to minimise face- to-face contact. The death certificate can then be applied for online and sent to you or your professional advisor.

The procedure normally is that the registrar will require a medical certificate of the cause of death. Usually, this is sent directly to the registrar and all you need do is make an appointment.

The registrar will require details of the date and place of birth and whether the deceased was or had been married. As a precaution if you hold the will make sure the names that you register are the same as the names on the will as you may have problems later when making an application for probate.

You will have to personally check the details and sign plus paying the fee. Obtain further copies of the death certificate as necessary. The death certificate is a certified copy of the entry of death on the register. Each copy will be around £7.00 (this can change between local authority areas and should be checked with your local registry office).

Disposal of the body

The body cannot be disposed of until the death has been registered and a green disposal certificate authorising whether it is a burial or cremation is obtained. If the coroner is involved there may be delay in the registration of the death. Any wishes by the deceased as to the disposal of the body is merely a wish and is not legally binding but most executors will respect the deceased's wishes

Funeral

It is not technically part of the executor's duties to arrange a funeral but the executor has the duty to dispose of the body. As he will be responsible for the costs out of the estate it is usual for the executor to at least be consulted. The direct costs of the funeral such as church, cemetery and cremation fees will be testamentary and administration expenses but not refreshments for mourners. Any payment for those out of the estate will need the permission of the residuary beneficiaries.

Burial

The funeral director makes arrangement for the burial of the body. Bodies may be buried elsewhere with permission of the local authority. Headstones may only be erected with the permission of the priest in charge, there is no automatic right to a headstone. Again, the cost of the headstone will not normally be regarded as a testamentary expense. Care should be taken before disposing of all the assets of the estate that sufficient money has been held back to pay for this at a later date. An estimate will be given but a margin should be retained as it is very embarrassing at a later date to have to ask the beneficiaries to pay when they think the estate has been wound up.

Dealing with assets where no grant is required

These include

1.   Nominated property
2.   Property held on a joint tenancy: this would include land, bank accounts and building society accounts. Joint shareholdings.
3.   Life policies written in trust. Although it can be transferred immediately it does not mean that it will not be subject to Inheritance tax if it comes within the tax limit.

Obtaining the will

Solicitors and banks will only normally require production of the Will on production of the death certificate and authority from the executors. Care should be taken that it is the last Will. With the executors' instructions you should send copies of the Will to the residuary beneficiaries.

Taking possession of the deceased persons estate

You should take possession of anything of a financial nature relating to the deceased's estate which ranges from actual cash to title deeds.

It is good practice when receiving items from the relatives to produce a comprehensive checklist. Send a copy of the schedule to the relatives as soon as possible. This will form the basis of the estate account. Also, it will resolve any future problems as you can quite rightly claim that you only have possession of the items that are on the checklist.

Try not to take possession of items that will give you problems in storing, as the beneficiaries will look to you to keep them safe. Give back all bags, cases etc as otherwise your office/home will end up looking like a left luggage office and you will never know if ever when or how to dispose of these items. They may turn out to be family heirlooms.

If any items are collected during the administration, be absolutely scrupulous about asking for receipts before they leave your possession. If in doubt about anyone's authority or identity make sure you check it before parting with the items. These are all precautions to keep down any potential complaints.

There are circumstances when assets may turn up later and an amended account can be submitted to HMRC. You should impress on the executors / administrators their duty to give a full and frank disclosure of the estate to HM Revenue and Customs, similarly with their duty to the beneficiaries.

The more detailed and evidential your account the less likely you are to have an enquiry from HMRC if all values are backed up by professional and current valuations.

<u>Practical considerations</u>

1.   secure any freehold or leasehold property. Obtain keys arrange for them to be locked etc.

2.   disconnect utilities and inform utility companies such as water gas electricity.

3.   check all deliveries have been stopped or post-redirected.

<u>Insurance</u>

Check there is an insurance policy in existence and contact insurance company about the interim arrangements.

Powers of Personal representatives before the grant

<u>Executors</u>

An executor's powers come from the death and the Will. The grant of probate is merely a confirmation to those powers. In reality the power is restricted by the fact that any other parties holding the assets will not release the money until a grant of probate has been produced.

<u>Administrators</u>

Their powers derive from the grant of administration; therefore they do not have the powers of an executor. It is important that the administrator does not intermeddle with the estate as otherwise he will not be able to renounce afterwards.

Certain basic activities such as insuring the property and feeding animals would be regarded as necessary and not intermeddling.

Vesting

Property vests in the executor immediately but not with the administrator. Obviously on the sale of property such as land the purchaser will expect to see the grant of probate even though it automatically vests in the executor.

Ascertaining the assets and liabilities.

Good practice is to use a checklist and examples as follows:

1.   Will

Where kept

Letter of Authority to release

Name & Address of Executors

1)   ....   2)...........................

....

....

3)   ....   4)...........................

....

No Will

Entitlement to estate...

Name & Address of Administrators

1)……………………………………………………….

2. Particulars of Deceased

Full Name…………………………………………………….

Alias……………………………………………………..

Date of Death   ………………….   Date of Birth…………..

Last Usual Address…………………………………………..

Married Status: Married / Single / Divorced / Widowed

Occupation……………………………………………….

Surviving Relatives:

Spouse [] Children   [   ] Parents [   ]

Domicile:

England & Wales   [   ] Scotland   [   ]

Wales   [   ]

National Insurance

Number………………………………………………………

Accountant:

Name………………………………………………………

Address……………………………………………………….

Stockbroker / Financial Advisor

Name……………………………………………………….

Address……………………………………………………….

Bank Details

Name   ………………………………   Account no………

Address……………………………………………………….

Joint Property Asset:

House] Bank a/c] Investments [

Description…………………………………………………….

Joint Holder…………………………………………………….

Joint Tenants   [   ]   Tenants in Common   [

See overleaf for schedule of assets and debts.

Schedule of assets and debts

Asset	Probate Value £	Corrected Value £	Grant Registered	Proceeds £
Stocks Shares				
National Savings Certificates				
Building Society a/c				
Current a/c Bank				
Deposit a/c Bank				
Premium Bonds				
Life Policies Bonds				
Freehold Property				
Leasehold Property				

Debts

Creditor Name	Nature of Debt	Amount £	Corrected Amount £	Date Paid
Utilities				
Inland Revenue				
Funeral A/c				

This checklist can immediately form the basis of the estate account and can be split into assets and liabilities.

VALUING THE ESTATE

Letters should be sent to all holders of assets that need valuation

The letter should ask:

1.   Details of the asset i.e., how much is in the account.

2.   Any income that has accrued since death such as interest.

3.   Send a copy of the death certificate as banks will normally expect to see this.

4.   Ask for any forms which may become necessary to sell or close the account for signature by the executors after the grant of probate.

Bank and building society accounts

You will need to ask the following:

1.   Balance plus interest if any
2.   Details of any other accounts
3.   Any items held on safe deposit.
4.   Details of any standing orders or any money received after date of death which may need to be refunded such as pension payments.
5.   You may need to borrow the IHT liability so ask them for any details that they might want.

Banks and building societies are more liberal about this and it is better to ask for money in the existing account if this is possible. If not, a loan will need to be set up.

Stocks and shares

A list of all the shares should be set up. You need to be meticulous with the actual share certificates that you take possession of. Make sure you create a schedule and get the executors or informants to sign the list by way of confirmation that is all they have given you.

People are exceedingly lax with certificates. And arguments can arise later as to what originals you possess. Obtain valuation from a stockbroker for which a fee is payable. Take instructions from the beneficiaries if at some date they wish them to be sold.

National Savings

Make application to the Director of Savings to obtain a valuation and forms to cash the holdings if necessary.

Building society accounts

Similar letter as to bank.

Social security /Pension

Letter to local office ask for balances or amounts owed.

Private Pension scheme

As above

Life Assurance

Obtain value of policy

Obtain Claim form

Land

An estate agent's valuation. Unless it is a farm then a full professional valuation is needed as you may be claiming a relief.

It is possible for the executors to give a valuation but the district valuer will be keen to be involved. Also, you need to be aware that for Capital Gains Tax purposes that the value at death will be the start value for the beneficiaries if the property is sold at a later date or transferred by way of assent. It is therefore important to get this right even if no IHT is payable. It will be much more difficult many years later to do a back calculation.

Remind beneficiaries of this so that you are not involved in hours of abortive work at some future date.

Funeral expenses

It is good practice to ask the holders of any funds to pay the funeral account. This has a double effect. It removes any embarrassment by the beneficiaries as the funeral director may contact them. It helps the funeral directors cash flow and cuts down any further administration by you.

Council Tax

There will be an exemption so write to the council immediately if the property is empty.

All other debts

Write and ask for accounts and state you will pay them once probate has been granted and the funds are available.

HM Customs and Excise

If the deceased had an accountant supply him with a copy of death certificate and ask for his requirements.

Statutory advertisements

By advertising, a personal representative will discharge his duty for payment of accounts not known by him.

*

<u>Searches</u>

Should you do a bankruptcy search against the deceased? Similarly, you may wish to make a bankruptcy search against any large beneficiaries as if you pay them the money and not their trustee in bankruptcy you may not have discharged your duty.

The Executors may be liable if property / money is handed to someone who is bankrupt. They cannot give a valid receipt

Taxation of the Estate

There are three taxes that could affect the estate.

1.   Income Tax
2.   Capital Gains Tax
3.   Inheritance Tax

The personal representatives are under a duty to deal with the deceased's tax affairs and settle any outstanding liabilities and claim any rebates that may be necessary.

If the estate is large enough, they will have to complete and submit the Inheritance Tax Account before probate or Letters of Administration will be granted.

In the event of inheritance tax to be paid, this will have to be paid before the grant is made.

Income tax

A return must be made to HMRC with the deceased's income up to the date of the death. The personal representative therefore should write to HMRC firstly to report the death and secondly to obtain a return to discover whether any tax may be due or owed to the estate.

The estate is entitled to the full personal reliefs for the tax year in question regarding the death.

Income received

Income received during the administration period.

There may be income that is being received during the administration period, such as salary, rent, dividends and interest on any investments.

Estate Income

This is income received during the administration period and finishes on the day when the value of the residuary estate is calculated for distribution purposes.

The personal representative must pay income tax received during the administration period although there are no personal reliefs.

The only advantage is that the estate in not liable for a higher rate tax which is currently 40%. There is relief for any interest paid and may arise as a result of obtaining allowance for the inheritance tax.

Capital Gains Tax

The personal representatives must settle any Capital gains tax payable on any gains made during the deceased's lifetime. There is no Capital gains tax liability just as a result of the death and the personal representatives and beneficiaries ultimately are treated as acquiring the assets on the deceased's death, at their market value at the date of death. It can therefore be very important to have a correct valuation of assets even though inheritance tax may not be payable, this will be the starting point for the beneficiaries in any future capital gains tax liability.

Inheritance Tax Exemptions

As we have seen, Inheritance tax is payable on the value of all the property that the deceased owned, up to the date of death. This includes property passing under his will, or under the intestacy rules as well as property held under a joint tenancy and nominated property. There are important exemptions, depending on who is the beneficiary, and no inheritance tax will be payable in the following circumstances.

- Spouse of a deceased
- A Charity
- A Political party
- Some national bodies such as museums and art galleries

Inheritance tax may be avoided is there is business property or agricultural property relief and inheritance tax may be payable if the deceased has died within seven years of making a lifetime gift. There is however tapering relief over the seven-year period.

Raising funds for paying the IHT on the personality

It is possible to pay instalments on land but not on the personal possessions. This must be paid before the grant is made so you may have to borrow the tax before you have access to the funds. Once borrowed or accessed the cheque will usually be in favour of HMRC.

Building Societies

This could be your best source of funds as they may allow you to have a cheque with only forms signed by the executors.

Direct Payment Scheme

Banks are now more amenable to paying the money direct to HMRC which is only fair as it is the deceased's money and therefore the estates.

****

Chapter 5

Making the Application for Probate-After the Grant-Distribution of the Estate

---

Applying for Probate

Having carried out a thorough appraisal of the estate, it is now time to make the application for probate.

Probate represents the official proof of the validity of a will and is granted by the court on production by the executors of the estate of the necessary documents. Only when probate is obtained are executors free to administer and distribute the estate. If the value of the estate is under £5000 in total, it may be possible to administer the estate without obtaining probate. Generally, if the estate is worth more than £5000, you will have to apply for probate (of the will) or letters of administration. There are a number of reasons for this:

- Banks, building societies and National Savings are governed by the Administration of Estates (Small payments) Act 1965. This only allows them to refund individual accounts up to £5000 without production of probate. However, Although the administration of Estates (Small Payments) Act 1965 sets out a threshold of only £5000, almost every bank or building society and financial institution will set their own limit to determine the point at which they will voluntarily release assets without a grant of representation (Grant of Probate if there is a Will or Grant Of Letter Of Administration if there is no Will) needing to be produced.

- You cannot sell stocks, shares, or land from an estate without probate, except in the case of land held in names of joint tenants where this passes on after death
- If the administration is disputed or if a person intends to make a claim as a dependant or member of the family, his or her claim is 'statute barred' six months after the grant of probate. The right to take action remains open if the estate is administered without probate
- A lay executor who managed to call in the assets of an estate without probate might miss the obligation to report matters to HMRC for inheritance tax purposes, especially where a substantial gift had been made in the seven years prior to the death.

Letters of administration

If someone dies intestate (without making a will) the rules of intestacy laid down by Act of Parliament will apply. An administrator must apply for letters of administration for exactly the same reasons as the executor applies for probate. The grant of letters of administration will be made to the first applicant. If a will deals with part only but not all of the administration (for example where the will defines who receives what but does not name an executor) the person entitled to apply for letters of administration makes the application to the Registrar attaching the will at the same time. The applicant is granted 'Letters of administration with will attached'.

Applying for letters of administration

The following demonstrates the order of those entitled to apply:

- The surviving spouse/civil partner (not unmarried partner)
- The children or their descendants (once over 18)
- If there are no children or descendants of those children who are able to apply, the parents of the deceased can apply
- Brothers and sisters 'of the half blood'
- Grandparents
- Aunts and uncles of the whole blood
- Aunts and uncles of the half blood
- The Crown (or Duchy of Lancaster or Duchy of Cornwall) if there are no blood relations.

Where the estate is insolvent other creditors have the right to apply.

The Probate Registry – applying for probate

The first step is to obtain the necessary forms. These can be downloaded from:

https://www.gov.uk/applying-for-probate/apply-for-probate.

There is also the (now preferred) facility to carry out the probate function online (see below) which is more relevant now following the pandemic and the associated backlog.

The executor will complete and send in the forms, they are checked and the amount of probate fees and inheritance tax assessed. The registry officials prepare the official document which the executor then swears (can be done online). The process from submission to swearing usually takes three to four weeks.

Filling in the forms

The necessary forms for applying for probate are:

- Form PA1P – the probate application form if a person left a will
- Form PA1A if a person did not leave a will
- Form 1HT 205 – the return of assets and debts

Examples of these forms are shown in the Appendix.

With the forms you will receive other items which serve as guidance to the forms and process:

- 1HT 206 – notes to help you with 1HT 205
- Form PA3 – a list of probate fees
- Form PA4 – Directory of Probate Registries

Form PA1P is uncomplicated. The form is split into white and blue sections with the applicant filling in the white sections. The form will ask which office the applicant wants to attend, details of the deceased, the will and something about you. In cases where more than one executor is involved, the registrar will usually correspond with one executor only. The form also has a space for naming any executors who cannot apply for probate, e.g., because they do not want to or have died since the will was written. If they may apply at a later date, the probate office will send an official 'power reserved letter' which the non-acting executor signs. This is a useful safeguard in case the first executor dies or becomes incapacitated before grant of probate is obtained.

You do not have to sign form PA1P. At the end of the process, the probate registry will couch the information you supply in legal jargon for the document you are required to sign.

Form PA1P contains a reminder that you must attach the death certificate, the will and the completed IHT form. If this form demonstrates that the estate exceeds the 'excepted estate' threshold (for inheritance tax purposes) form 1HT 200 will have to be completed.

Probate Fees

The proposals for a significant hike in probate fees have been scrapped. The fee for initial probate is £273 (2022/2023), although there is no fee if the estate is valued at less than £5,000. You must enclose a cheque for the application fee if applying by post. You can pay for extra official copies of the grant of representation, which may be used to send to institutions in place of the original grant (an ordinary copy is not acceptable for this purpose).

The fee for each official copy is £1.50p a copy if you request it with the application. For more details of probate fees go to HM Courts and Tribunals Service form PA3

Probate online
The Probate Service accepts online applications from personal applicants and a small number of pre-selected solicitors based on the criteria below:

- applications where up to 4 executors are applying
- there is an original will available even if the person who died made changes to that will (these changes are known as codicils)
- the person who has died classed England and Wales as their permanent home or intended to return to England and Wales to live permanently.

Online applications are now the preferred process because of COVID 19 and its aftermath.

What the online application provides
The online application form includes:

- a new statement of truth for you to declare that the information provided is correct, which removes the need for you to swear an oath in person
- the function to pay the fee online removing the need to post a cheque to the Probate Service

- a 'save and return' function allows you to save and revisit an application if you need to find further information. This allows a part-finished application to be saved and completed later.

What is required in order to submit an online application?

The online application form is easier to understand but you will still be required to provide supporting documents as per the current process. These are:

- the original will and two photocopies
- an official copy of the death certificate
- the associated inheritance tax forms and figures
- any other supporting documents relevant to the case (e.g., a renunciation form)

Alternatively - Sending the forms

If the estate you are administering can be contained on form 1HT 205, you are ready to send in your application. Make sure that you take photocopies of all material. You should send the following:

- The will
- The death certificate
- Probate application form PA1P or PA1A
- Short form 1HT 205
- A cheque for the fee (you can pay online before sending the papers)

Send to:

HMCTS Probate

PO Box 12625

Harlow

CM20 9QE

Use a signed-for or tracked postal service that will deliver to PO boxes to send your documents. The death certificate will be returned to you but the will and any updates to it will not be.

Letters of administration

If the deceased has left no will, then the next of kin will apply for a grant of letters of administration instead of probate. The same is the case if a will was left but no executors appointed. In these cases, the grant is called 'letters of administration with will annexed'. When letters of administration are sought, the administrators may in some cases have to provide a guarantee – for example where the beneficiaries are underage or mentally disabled or when the administrator is out of the country.

The guarantee is provided by an insurance company at a cost or by individuals who undertake to make good – up to the gross value of the estate – any deficiency caused by the administrators failing in their duties. Letters of administration may also be taken out by creditors of an estate if executors deliberately do not apply for probate – for instance, if the estate has insufficient assets to pay all creditors and legatees.

The grant of probate

There may be a time lapse of six weeks or more (due to the current backlog caused by coronavirus) between lodging the probate papers and the grant of probate. After this has happened, however, things move quickly. If there is no inheritance tax to be paid – where the net estate is less than £325,000, or where the deceased property goes to the spouse – the grant of probate (or letters of administration) is issued.

If inheritance tax is due, it takes two to three weeks before the exact amount is calculated and the grant is usually ready about several weeks later.

The grant of probate is signed by an officer of the probate registry. Attached to the grant of probate is a photocopy of the will. (All original wills are kept at the Principal Probate Registry in London). Each page of your copy of the will carries the impress of the courts official seal. It is accompanied by a note which explains the procedure for collecting and distributing the estate and advises representatives to take legal advice in the event of dispute or other difficulty.

Procedure for obtaining probate where the tax situation is more complicated

Although the procedure for obtaining a grant of probate, a grant of letters of administration or a grant of letters of administration with will annexed are similar, the procedure concerning inheritance tax accounts is rather more complicated. There are three types of inheritance tax account, with different forms in each case. They are as follows:

- If the deceased lived abroad and he or she has few assets in the UK, then form IHT207 will usually be the one to use. In some cases, form IHT 400 must be used but form IHT 207 will make this clear.
- If the deceased was domiciled in the United Kingdom then form IHT 205 is the usual form to use where the gross value of the estate does not exceed the excepted estate limit, which is the inheritance tax threshold (currently £325,000) unless a grant of probate is applied for before 6th of August in the tax year in which the death took place, in which case the excepted estate limit is the inheritance tax limit set for the previous tax year

The Chancellor announced, in the July 2015 budget, that he was increasing the IHT allowance to £1m (for a couple) for the family home. People will not have to pay IHT on properties worth less than £1million. This was phased in from April 2017. However, there are a few things to note. The 'Family Homes Allowance' applies only to property left to direct descendants, children, grandchildren, great grandchildren and so on. Stepchildren will also count. The allowance will not apply to indirect descendants such as nieces and nephews. It is also suggested that advice should be sought when thinking of downsizing as the new IHT rules may affect your tax liabilities.

Recent developments

Since April 2018, anyone leaving a home, or a share of a home, to direct descendants (children, grandchildren etc) was entitled to an additional Inheritance Tax exemption of up to £150,000. This increased to £175,000 in April 2020.

The gross value of a person's estate is the total value of his assets together with the value of any gifts made by him (a) in the seven years before his death or (b) from which he continued to benefit and upon which he had elected not to pay the pre-owned assets income tax charge or (c) from which he had reserved a benefit.

Form IHT 400 should be used if:

- the deceased was domiciled in the United Kingdom but his estate does not fall within the above classes
- the estate includes an alternatively secured
- pension, that is, a pension benefit in a pension scheme registered under section 153 of the Finance Act 2004 which has been earmarked to provide benefits for a person over the age of 75 but not used to provide pension benefits or an annuity for him
- the deceased had an unsecured benefit from a pension scheme registered under section 153 of the Finance Act 2004 and he acquired the benefit as a dependent of a person who died aged 75 or over
- the deceased had not taken his full retirement benefits before he died from a personal pension policy or a pension scheme of which he was a member and when he was in poor

health, he changed the policy or scheme so as to make a change in or to dispose of the benefits to which he was entitled

- the deceased ever bought an annuity and within seven years of his death paid premiums for a life assurance policy of which the policy monies were not payable to his estate, his spouse or civil partner
- the deceased had a right to benefit from assets held in a trust (other than assets held in a single trust which do not exceed £150,000)
- within seven years of his death the deceased gave up a right to benefit from assets valued at more than £150,000 held in trust
- within seven years of his death the deceased made gifts (other than normal birthday, festive, marriage or civil partnership gifts not exceeding £3000 per year) totalling over £150,000
- the deceased made a gift after 18th March 1986 from which he continued to benefit or in respect of which the person who received the gift did not take full possession of it
- the deceased had made an election that the pre-owned assets income charge should not apply to assets he had previously owned or to the cost of which he had contributed and in either case from which he had continued to benefit
- the deceased lived abroad and form IHT 207 is not appropriate

- the deceased owned or benefited from assets outside the United Kingdom worth more than £100,000
- the estate intends to claim and benefit from any unused nil-rate inheritance tax band of a spouse or civil partner who has died before the deceased (this is done by completing form IHT 402 and returning it with the completed form IHT 400.

For more details about IHT 400 go to:
www.gov.uk/government/publications/inheritance-tax-inheritance-tax-account-iht400

Distributing an estate in accordance with the law of intestacy
If someone dies without making a will, he is said to die intestate and his estate is inherited according to the law of intestacy. Intestacy law divides relatives into groups or classes according to their blood relationships to the deceased. All members of a given class inherit in equal shares. There is a specific order in which the various classes inherit and if all members of a given class have died before the deceased without leaving issue who survived the deceased, the next class inherits. The words 'child' and 'children' are used to mean a person's immediate dependents (as opposed to grandchildren) and do not include a stepchild or stepchildren, but no distinction is made before legitimate and illegitimate children. Adopted children inherit from their adoptive parents and not from their birth parents. If those entitled to inherit are under 18, then the inheritance is

held in trust for them, until they either reach the age of 18, marry or enter into a registered civil partnership.

To decide who is entitled to inherit, look for the first class and if there is no member of the class who survived the deceased or predeceased him look for those in the next class.

If a person dies without leaving a will or without leaving a valid will, the laws of intestacy apply. It is important to note that the Inheritance and Trustees Power Act 2014 introduced changes regarding who will inherit under and intestate estate and also how much they inherit. The changes will have no effect on people who die with assets worth less than £250,000.

The law of intestacy rests on the question of: who survived the deceased? If there is a lawful spouse or civil partner and the deceased died leaving children then the spouse receives the first £250,000 in respect of assets solely in the deceased's name plus half of the remaining capital. Children receive half remaining capital, then on the death of the spouse/civil partner the children receive the remaining capital. If there is a lawful spouse/civil partner and the deceased died leaving no children, the spouse receives the entire estate. This is a new provision introduced following the introduction of the above-mentioned Inheritance and Trustees Powers Act 2014, which came into force in October 2014.

The changes apply in England and Wales.

-If there are children, but no spouse or civil partner, everything goes to the children in equal shares.

Further:

-If there are parent(s) but no spouse or civil partner or children then everything goes to parents in equal shares.

-If there are brothers or sisters, but no spouse or civil partner, or children or parents everything goes to brothers and sisters of the whole blood equally.

-If there are no brothers or sisters of the whole blood, then all goes to brothers and sisters of the half blood equally.

-If there are grandparents, but no spouse or civil partner, or children or parents, or brothers and sisters everything goes to the grandparents equally.

-If there are uncles and aunts, but no spouse or civil partner, or children or parents, or brothers or sisters or grandparents, then everything goes to uncles and aunts of the whole blood equally.

-If there are no uncles and aunts of the whole blood then all goes to uncles and aunts of the half blood equally.

-If there is no spouse or civil partner and no relatives in any of the categories shown above then everything goes to the Crown.

-A spouse is a person who was legally married to the deceased when he or she died.

-A civil partner is someone who was in a registered civil partnership with the deceased when he or she died. It doesn't include people simply living together as unmarried partners or as common law husband and wife.

-The term children includes children born in or out of wedlock and legally adopted children; it also includes adult sons and daughters. It does not, however, include stepchildren.

-Brothers and sisters of the whole blood have the same mother and father. Brothers and sisters of the half blood (more commonly referred to as half brothers and sisters) have just one parent in common.

-Uncles and aunts of the whole blood are brothers and sisters of the whole blood of the deceased's father or mother.

-Uncles and aunts of the half blood are brothers and sisters of the half blood of the deceased's father or mother.

It is important to note that if any of the deceased children die before him/her, and leave children of their own (that is grandchildren of the deceased) then those grandchildren between them take the share that their mother or father would have taken if he or she had been alive. This also applies to brothers and sisters and uncles and aunts of the deceased who have children – if any of them dies before the deceased, the share that he or she would have had if he or she were still alive, goes to his or her children between them.

The principle applies through successive generations – for example a great grandchild will take a share of the estate if his father and his grandfather (who were respectively the grandson and son of the deceased) both died before the deceased.

It is important to note that if any of the following situations apply to you, or if you are in any doubt whatsoever, you should seek legal advice before distributing the estate of a person who has died without leaving a will:

- The deceased died before 4th of April 1988
- Anyone entitled to a share of the estate is under 18
- Someone died before the deceased and the share he or she would have had goes to his or her children instead
- The spouse/civil partner dies within 28 days of the deceased.

A spouse or civil partner must outlive the deceased by 28 days before they become entitled to any share of the estate. An ex-wife or civil partner (who was legally divorced from the deceased or whose civil partnership with the deceased was dissolved before the date of death) gets nothing from the estate under the rules of intestacy, but he/she may be able to make a claim under the inheritance (Provision for Family and Dependants) Act 1975, through the courts.

Legal advice should be sought if making such a claim. Anyone who is under 18 (except a spouse or civil partner of the deceased) does not get his or her share of the estate until he or she becomes 18 or marries under that age. It must be held on trust for him or her until he or she becomes 18 or gets married. Apart from the spouse or civil partner of the deceased, only blood relatives, and those related by legal adoption, are entitled to share in the estate. Anyone else who is related through marriage and not by blood is not entitled to a share in the estate.

If anyone who is entitled to a share of the estate dies after the deceased but before the estate is distributed, his or her share forms part of his or her own estate and is distributed under the terms of his or her will or intestacy. Great uncles and great aunts of the deceased (that is brothers and sisters of his or her grandparents) and their children are not entitled to a share in the estate.

Further changes under the Inheritance and Trustees Powers Act 2014

The definition of personal property/chattels has also changed. Under old rules, the term "chattels" was outdated and included old-fashioned terms such as "carriages", "linen" and "scientific instruments". Under new rules "personal chattels" includes all tangible moveable property, apart from property which consists of money or security for money, or property that was used solely or mainly for business purposes or was held solely as an investment.

The old definition of chattels will still apply where a Will was executed before 1 October 2014 and refers to s55 (1) (x) (Administration of Estates Act 1925). Under old rules, if an individual died leaving a child under the age of 18, who was subsequently adopted by someone else, there was a risk that the child may lose their inheritance from their natural parent. The new rules ensure that children will not lose any claim to inheritance if they were adopted after the death of a natural parent.

**

Various points concerning distributions of the estate

Children conceived by artificial insemination or in vitro fertilisation

When distributing to those known to have been conceived by artificial insemination or by in vitro fertilisation the following should be borne in mind: Except for inheritance of titles and land which devolves with titles, if a child is artificially conceived as above:

- In the case of a couple who are married and not judicially separated, the husband is considered to be the father unless it can be proved that he did not consent to the conception
- In the case of treatment provided for a man and woman together, the man is considered to be the father irrespective of whether or not his sperm was used
- The mother is the woman who has carried the child as the result of the placing in her of an embryo or of an egg or sperm.

Although the Human Fertilisation and Embryology (Deceased Fathers) Act 2003 permits a deceased husband or partner to be registered as the father of a child conceived after his death by the use of his sperm, the registration does not give the child any rights of inheritance.

Underage beneficiaries

Unless permitted to do so by the will, neither a person under the age of 18 nor that person's parent or guardian can give a valid receipt for the capital of the bequest (as opposed to the income that it produces) and cannot give a valid discharge for any capital payment made to him. A valid receipt for income produced by a bequest to a person who is under the age of 18 can only be given by the person, or his parent or guardian, if the beneficiary is married or in a registered civil partnership.

Accordingly, a personal representative should not make any capital payment to a minor, or an income payment to an unmarried minor who is not in a registered civil partnership unless authorised by the will. The money should be either held on trust until of age or paid into court.

Bankrupts and those of unsound mind

Payments should not be made to a beneficiary who is bankrupt. Similarly, if a bequest has been made to a person who is not believed to be of sound mind, the bequest should not be made to that person personally but to his deputy appointed by the court of protection or to his attorney appointed by an enduring power of attorney made by him before 1st October 2007 or a lasting power of attorney. In the case of both types of power of attorney the powers must have been registered with the Public Guardian and made before the beneficiary lost his sanity.

Beneficiaries who cannot be found

There may be cases where it is difficult to trace a beneficiary, even though every effort may have been made, such as advertising in the local paper or even national papers. If executors do not personally know a beneficiaries address or whereabouts then other exhaustive searches will have to be made, such as the local telephone directory where the beneficiary lives There are other avenues which can be explored. One is that of Traceinline on 02392 988 966 www.traceinline.co.uk. They can trace beneficiaries if the executor can supply the person's name and date of birth. A fee is payable. Traceline will also inform the executor if the beneficiary has died. There is a fee to be paid so it is only worth it if there is significant money and assets at stake.

Probate Fees

Proposals for a significant hike in probate fees have been scrapped. The fee for initial probate is £273, although there is no fee if the estate is valued at less than £5,000. You must enclose a cheque for the application fee if applying by post (although there is a facility to pay online as described earlier). You can pay for extra official copies of the grant of representation, which may be used to send to institutions in place of the original grant (an ordinary copy is not acceptable for this purpose).

The fee for each official copy is £1.50p a copy if you request it with the application. For more details of probate fees go to HM Courts and Tribunals Service form PA3

****

Schedule of Standard Probate Letters

(See overleaf)

1. Letter to Debtors

2. Letter to Creditors

3. Letter to Bank applying for payment of Funeral Account

4. Letter to Bank applying for payment of Inheritance Tax

5. Letter to Capital Taxes re Inheritance Tax

6. Letter to Probate Registry for Grant of Probate

7. Letter to Bank or Building Society collecting funds

8. Authority for receiving money

9. Letter to Registrar to transfer shares

10. Letter paying bills from the Estate

11. Letter to Beneficiaries with statement for approval

12. Letter sending Pecuniary Legacy

13. Receipt for Pecuniary Legacy *(on behalf of ....)*

14. Receipt for Pecuniary Legacy

15. Letter to Beneficiary

16. Receipt for Beneficiary

17. Instruction sheet for a Will

****

STANDARD LETTERS

Please note that these are for guidance only and may change depending on the circumstances.

## 1.	Letter to Debtors

Any date

Address

Dear Sirs

**Re	*Name* – deceased**
**	*Description***
**	Account No:**

We enclose certified copy of the Death Certificate of the above and should be obliged if you would let us know the amount outstanding to the credit of this account including interest accrued but not credited at the date of death.

Probate will be registered with you in due course.

If you have any form or if you require authority for the Executors to sign to let us have any proceeds, repayments, or monies due to the Estate could you please let us have such forms.

Alternatively, please confirm at this stage exactly what authority you will require. This should save delays once Probate has been granted.

Yours faithfully

2.   Letter to Creditors

Any date

Customer Services
Address

Dear Sirs

Re   *Name*   deceased
**   Account Number:**

We act on behalf of the Estate of the above unfortunately ………..
died   on   the
……………. we enclose a copy of the death certificate for your
information and retention.

We would be obliged if you would kindly forward all future
accounts to ourselves. We are currently making application for
Probate, once this is available, we will pay all outstanding
accounts.

Yours faithfully

3.   Letter to Bank Applying for Payment of Funeral Account

Any date

Bank/Building Society
Address

Dear Sirs

Re   *Name*   –   deceased
Address:
Account No:

As you are aware we act on behalf of the Estate of the Late
....

We enclose a copy of the funeral account and we would be obliged if it is at all possible for you to draw a cheque in favour of .... to pay this account. If you require any forms to be signed by our client, please do not hesitate to contact us.

Your assistance is appreciated

Yours faithfully

4.　Letter to Bank applying for payment of Inheritance Tax

Any date

Bank
Address

Dear Sirs

Re ……………….　　　　　—　　　　　**deceased**

　　　Account No: …………………..

As you are aware we act for the Estate of the Late ……………….

There is a small amount of £……….. due for Inheritance Tax and we would be obliged if it is at all possible for you to draw a cheque in favour of Her Majesty's Revenue and Customs to pay the amount due.

If you require any forms to be signed by the Executors please do not hesitate to contact us.

Your assistance is appreciated.

Yours faithfully

5.   Letter to Capital Taxes re Inheritance Tax

Any date

Capital Taxes Offices

Dear Sirs

Re   *Name* – deceased

We take this opportunity of enclosing the following:

1. A cheque in the sum of £??????? - the total amount of Inheritance Tax due

2. IHT200

3. D1

4. D7

5. D10

6. D13

7. D17

8. D18

We would be obliged if the D18 could be receipted and returned to us in due course.

Yours faithfully

6. Letter to Probate Registry for Grant of Probate

Any date

Ipswich District Probate Registry

8 Arcade Street

Ipswich

Suffolk IP1 1EJ

Dear Sirs

Re   Name – deceased

We enclose the following to lead to a Grant of Probate of the will of the above:

1. Oath for Executors

2. Will dated ?????

3. *Form IHT205 signed by the Executors*

     or

4. *D18*

5. Cheque in the sum of £????

We await hearing from you once Probate has been granted.

Yours faithfully

7.   Letter to Bank or Building Society Collecting Funds

Any date
Bank/Building Society
Address

Dear Sirs

Re   *Name*   **deceased**
       Account No: ....

We take this opportunity of enclosing the following:

1.   Office Copy Probate – kindly return as soon as possible

2.   Authority Letter/Withdrawal form

We await hearing from you with the proceeds of the account.

Yours faithfully

8.   Authority for Receiving Money

Any date

Bank plc
Address

Dear Sirs

Re   ***Name***   –   **deceased**
      Address
      Account No: **Sort**   **Code:**
      Account No: **Sort Code:**

We hereby give you authority to let .... of .... have the proceeds due to the Estate of the Late ....

Signature   ....
                 Name:

Signature   ....
                 Name:

Dated   ....

9.   Letter to Registrar to Transfer Shares

Any date

Registrars
Address

Dear Sirs

Re   *Name*   –   deceased
…………………. Shares

We take this opportunity of enclosing the following:

1. Original Share Certificate

2. Stock Transfer Form duly signed by the Executors of the Estate

3. Office Copy Probate – Please return as soon as possible

We would be obliged if the Shares could be transferred into the name of …………..

Kindly confirm to us when this has been completed.

Yours faithfully

10.   Letter paying bills from the Estate

Any date

Address

Dear Sirs

Re   *Name*   —   **deceased**

Account Ref:

We take this opportunity of enclosing your account together with a cheque in the sum of £...............

Kindly return your account duly receipted in due course and we would be obliged if you would kindly confirm that there are no further outstanding sums and this account is clear.

Yours faithfully

11. Letter to Beneficiary with Statement for Approval

Any date

Beneficiary Name

Address

Dear ....

Re   *Name* – deceased

I take this opportunity of enclosing my statement of account. You will note that there is a retention of £............ which I will hold until I have confirmation that there are no further amounts due from the Estate.

If you would kindly confirm that the statement is in order, I will arrange for your share of the residuary Estate to be paid to you immediately.

Yours sincerely

12.   Letter Sending Pecuniary Legacy

Any dateAddress

Dear ....

Re   *Name – deceased*
        Address:

We act for the Estate of .... deceased. *Name of deceased* left you a legacy of £............ and we have pleasure in enclosing a cheque for that amount together with a receipt which please sign, date and return to me

Yours sincerely

13.   Receipt for Pecuniary Legacy *(on behalf of ……….)*

IN THE ESTATE OF ……………… - DECEASED

I …………………………………………. the Treasurer of ……………, *Address* acknowledge to have received from the Executors of *Name* deceased the sum of …….. Thousand ……… Hundred and ……… Pounds (£………) being the pecuniary legacy bequeathed to the ……… by his / her Will.

Dated   Any date

Signed ………………………………………

14.   Receipt for Pecuniary Legacy

IN THE ESTATE OF .... - DECEASED

I .... acknowledge to have received from the Executors of .... deceased the sum of .... Thousand .... Hundred and .... Pounds and (£...............) being the pecuniary legacy bequeathed to me by his / her Will.

Dated   Any date

Signed ....

15.   Letter to Beneficiary

Any date

Address

Dear ……………..

Re   *Name* – deceased

I take this opportunity of enclosing a cheque in the sum of £………. which is the amount due to you as one of the beneficiaries of the Estate. *I am holding a small retention of £……… for ……………..*

I also enclose a copy of the statement for your information and a receipt which please sign, date and return to me

Yours sincerely

16.   Receipt for Beneficiary

IN THE ESTATE OF ……………. - DECEASED

I …………………. acknowledge to have received from the Executors of

…………………. deceased the sum of ………… Pounds and …………
Pence (£……………..) being the share of the residuary Estate
bequeathed to me by his / her Will.

Dated   Any date

Signed ………………………………………

17.   Instruction Sheet for a Will

Full Name: ....

Address: ....

                                        ....

Telephone No: ....

Executors: ....

Addresses: ....

Alternative Executors: ....

Addresses: ....

Beneficiaries: ....

                        ....

Addresses: ....

            ....

(If the Beneficiaries are currently older than you, you may give consideration to appointing an alternative Beneficiary)

Alternative Beneficiaries: ....

Addresses   ....

Any Specific Item you wish to give away: ....

....

Any Specific Sums of Money you wish to give away: ....

....

....

Any other wishes you may have (such as either being buried or cremated)

....

....

Signed: ....

Dated: ....

GLOSSARY OF TERMS

A

Abatement -When the Estate has insufficient money to pay the bills, then any gifts will be reduced pro rata to make enough money to pay such bills, debts and expenses.

Ademption-If when the Will comes into effect, that is the date of the death, the gift does not exist, the gift lapses. It may have been sold or given away during the deceased's lifetime.

Administrator/Administrix-In the event of an Intestacy, this is a definition of a person who deals with the deceased's estate.

Assent-A document which transfer the freehold or leasehold property to the beneficiary.

Assets-Everything belonging to the deceased

Attestation Clause-A note at the end of the Will, confirming that the Will has been properly signed and witnessed.

B

Bankruptcy-When a person cannot pay their debts, they can apply to the Court to have themselves made bankrupt or you can make someone else bankrupt if you are a creditor. The bankrupts' affairs are then run by the Trustee in bankruptcy until they are discharged.

Beneficiary-beneficiary of a will

Bequeathed-Old fashioned word meaning – To leave someone property, more likely now to be bequest. A gift other than cash can be money or shares or other physical items.

Bona Vacantia-In the event of no other relative being alive, there is no one to inherit it goes to the Crown

C

Capacity-This means both mental and being of age that is 18 years old to be able to act as Executor or Administrator and a Beneficiary needs capacity to be able to receive the gift and give a valid receipt.

Capital Gains Tax (CGT)-When an asset has been owned during the deceased's lifetime and is sold for more than it was acquired for, then after deduction of allowances and reliefs, this tax is payable.

Caveat-A caution which will be given to the Probate Registry when there is doubt about the validity of the Will or whether there is a dispute about who is entitled to be the Executor.

Chargeable Gift-Anything left under the terms of the Will or during a person's lifetime, which is liable to tax.

Chattels-These are such things as pets, cars, boats, furniture, jewellery ornaments etc. Business assets money and securities are not chattels.

Children-The covers both legitimate and illegitimate children together with legally adopted children. This does not include stepchildren.

Codicil-An additional Will to make changes in your original Will.

Contentious Probate-Where someone lodges a caveat preventing the issue of a grant and their objections over such matters as the validity of the Will or the entitlement of someone to apply for the grant.

Continent Gift-Something left with a condition attached, which is an age or a condition.

Conveyancing-The process by which land and buildings are transferred.

Court of Protection-Any Power of Attorney either registered or unregistered or the persons affairs were with the Receivers then all such powers lapse on death.

D

Death Certificate-When a death is registered you should obtain extra copies for anyone who needs them. Most institutions want to see the original copy, not a photocopy.

Devise-Old fashioned word meaning to give

Deeds of Variation-If all the beneficiaries agree, then after the death, the terms of the Will may be altered, usually for the purpose of saving Inheritance Tax. It must be drawn up within two years of the date of death.

Distribution of the Estate-Once probate has been granted, and all monies have been collected it, all debts and taxes have been paid and the accounts agreed, then the Estate may be distributed.

Donation of Organs-The deceased may give directions for the disposal of their body. The decision is that of the Executors who will generally follow the wishes of the deceased

E

Enduring Power of Attorney (EPOA)-If an Enduring Power of Attorney was being used prior to death this will cease on death.

Engrossment-A final copy of a document.

Excepted Estate-These are estates under a certain limit that do not have to be notified to the Inland Revenue

Executor/Executrix-The Person named in the Will to deal with the deceased Estate.

G

Grant of Letter of Administration-This means the dealing with the deceased's Estate after death. The administration is undertaken by an Administrator if there is no Will or an Executor if there is a Will.

Grant of Probate-This is where there is a Will and an Executor has been appointed.

Guardians-People appointed by the Will, another parent, or the Court to act with parental responsibility for a child.

H

Half Blood-Where people share only one parent in common, they are of the half blood. For example, Brother of the half blood.

Headstones-Reasonable costs of the headstone can be deducted with the funeral from the Estate together with reasonable cost of the wake. Again, depending on the size of the Estate.

I

IHT-Inheritance Tax

Intestacy-Where no Will has been made

Intestate-The person who Dies without making a Will

Issue-Or living descendant

J

Joint Tenant-Usually the surviving spouse and the property automatically passes to the surviving spouse and there is an Inheritance Tax exemption.

Joint Assets-Two or more persons have a legal interest in a property, usually land and buildings. Normally, all the other joint owners inherit automatically. They are assessed for Inheritance Tax purposes, even though they pass automatically to the surviving joint owners. A proper valuation should be made.

L

Land Registry-Land Registry www.landreg.gov.uk.

Leasehold property-The Executor/Administrator retains any rights that the original Leaseholder would have had, such as being able to buy the freehold etc.

Legacy-A gift left to someone in a Will other than house or land.

Letter of Administration-Equivalent to the Grant of Probate where no Will has been made

Liabilities-Another word for debts. They need to be identified and show in any probate application. Any creditors will need to be informed and once funds have been gathered these debts should be paid off.

Life Interest-The right to enjoy the benefit for life.

M
Minor/Infant-Any child under the age of 18

N
Newspaper Advertisements-These involve Obituary Notices and Trustee Act Notices

O
Oath-An oath is a sworn statement, usually whilst holding the Bible but an affirmation of the truth can be made instead of swearing on the Bible.

Office Copy Entries-This is evidence of the property title at the Land Registry.

P

Pecuniary Legacy-Any Specific amount of money

Personal Representative-Can mean either the Executor or Administrator, just a general term to cover them both.

Probate-Confirmation that the Will is valid and the Executors have the authority to deal with the Estate

R

Renunciation-The Executor has the right to renounce, which means giving up his or her right to be the Executor. To renounce the Executor needs to sign a Form or Letter of Renunciation, which is then sent to the Probate Registry by the proving Executor

Residue-This is the Estate of the deceased, which remains after distribution to the beneficiaries after payment of all gifts and all taxes, debts etc.

Revocation of Will-This means to cancel any previously written Will. Usually, a new Will revokes a previously written Will or it can be revoked in other ways by destroying it etc.

S

Small Estate-Any Estate under the figure of £5000.00

Specific Legacy-A gift of some specific item such as a physical item – car or an amount of money

Spouse-Old legal term for a Wife or Husband.

Survivorship-Where two or more joint Tenants have outlived the deceased. The joint Tenant then inherits a share of the Estate automatically by survivorship. No probate needs to be proved.

T

Tenant-Either a joint tenant or tenant in common. Confusing to the public as this is nothing to do with leasehold property. Therefore, you can be a joint tenant or tenant in common of freehold property.

Tenants in common-This is where property is held by two or more people in different shares. Unless shown otherwise, it will usually be fifty/fifty like joint tenants. If one Tenant dies their share passes according to the Will.

Testamentary expenses-Reasonable costs incurred in the administration of the estate. Professional Executors are unable to receive compensation unless it is specific term of the Will.

Testator/Testatrix-This is a person making the Will. Testatrix is the female form.

Trust-An arrangement to hold property for another. The Trustee is not the legal owner.

Trustees-This is where somebody who is responsible to hold Trust assets on behalf of the beneficiaries.

U

Unregistered Land-Certain areas of land have not been registered as there has been no transfer or other variation of the Title. This is equally as affective as registered land but the Land Registry are changing the rules so within the foreseeable future, all land will become registered.

Undue Influence-Where pressure either mental or physical will be put on a party to do an act against their will.

Validity of Will-For a Will to be valid it has to be in writing, signed, witnessed correctly and the Testator must know he or she is signing.

W

Will-A formal document outlining who is to be your executor after death and to whom you leave possessions etc.

****

Useful Addresses

Department for National Savings

Glasgow G58 1SB

For enquiries about Capital Bonds, Children's Bonus Bonds, FIRST Option Bonds, Fixed Rate Savings Bonds, Ordinary Accounts, and Investment Accounts.

www.nsandi.com

Tel: 08085 007 007

Department for Work and Pensions

Caxton House

Tothill Street

London

SW1H 9NA

https://www.gov.uk/government/organisations/department-for-work-pensions

HM Revenue and Customs Capital Taxes Office

Tel: 0300 123 1072

The Law Society of England and Wales

www.lawsociety.org.uk

London Gazette

London

The London Gazette

PO Box 3584

Norwich NR7 7WD

T: +44 (0)333 200 2434

F: +44 (0)333 202 5080

E: london@thegazette.co.uk

Edinburgh

The Edinburgh Gazette

PO Box 3584

Norwich NR7 7WD

T: +44 (0)333 200 2434

F: +44 (0)333 202 5080

E: edinburgh@thegazette.co.uk

Belfast

The Belfast Gazette

TSO Ireland

19a Weavers Court, Weavers Court Business Park

Linfield Road

Belfast BT12 5GH

T: +44 (0)28 9089 5135

F: +44 (0)28 9023 5401

E: belfast@thegazette.co.uk

Solicitors Regulation Authority

The Cube

199 Wharfside Street

Birmingham B1 1RN

www.sra.org.uk

0370 606 2555

Information on solicitors specialising in wills and probate

The Principal Probate Registry

First Avenue House

42-49 High Holborn

London WC1V 6NP

Probate Helpline 0300 123 1072

Useful Addresses in Scotland

Accountant of Court

Scottish Courts and Tribunals Service

Saughton House

Broomhouse Drive

Edinburgh

EH11 3XD

Tel 0131 444 3300

Fax 0131 443 2610

enquiries@scotcourts.gov.uk

Law Society of Scotland

Atria One

144 Morrison Street

Edinburgh

EH3 8EX

0131 226 7411

www.lawscot.org.uk

Registers of Scotland

0800 169 9391

(Head Office)

ros.gov.uk

Sheriff Clerks Office

Commissary Department

27 Chambers Street

Edinburgh EH1 1LB-0131 225 2525

****

Index

****

Main Probate Forms for HMRC

1. IHT205 – Return of Estate Information
2. IHT400 – Inland Revenue Account for Inheritance Tax
3. IHTWS – Inheritance Tax work sheet

https://www.gov.uk/.../contact/probate-and-inheritance-tax-enquiries

General Probate Forms

The Following Probate Forms, covering the whole probate process, are obtainable on the website:

https://www.gov.uk/government/collections/probate-forms

1. Probate guidance and postal forms

2. Probate application: supporting forms

3. Stop and extend a grant of representation

4. Contest a will : forms and guidance

5. Deposit or withdraw your will from storage

6. Other probate services

7. Probate practitioner forms

Overleaf example form PA1P, apply for probate where there is a will and PA15 form of renunciation give up probate executor rights.

****

PA1P — Probate application

This form is for an application where the person who has died left a will

Checklist – before you send your application form to HMCTS Probate you will need to enclose the following. This checklist must be completed. If you do not enclose all of the required documents it will delay your application. Please keep copies of all documents that you send.

- [ ] PA1P - Probate Application (this form) - where a person who has died has left a will.
- [ ] Inheritance Tax Summary Form: Please submit the appropriate form (IHT205 or IHT207, and IHT217 if applicable), signed by all applicants (see additional notes in Section 7).
- [ ] The last original will and any codicils made since that will.
- [ ] A copy of any foreign wills or any wills dealing with assets held outside England and Wales (and if not in English, an English translation).
- [ ] An official copy (**not** a photocopy) of the death certificate, or a coroner's interim certificate of the person who has died.
- [ ] Any other documents requested on this form. Please list them:

As well as the application fee, there is a fee for each official copy of the Grant of Representation that we provide.

How many official copies of the Grant of Representation do you require for use **in** the United Kingdom?

How many official copies of the Grant of Representation do you require for use **outside** of the United Kingdom?

Application fee	£
Fees for copies	£
Total fees	£

- [ ] A cheque/postal order payable to '**HMCTS**' in respect of HMCTS's fees. Please write the name of the person who has died on the back of the cheque.

SECTION A – PERSONAL INFORMATION

Please complete in BLOCK capitals placing a tick in boxes where applicable.

1. **About the applicant(s)** – All applicants must be over 18 years and a maximum of 4 may apply

1.1 Title and full name including middle names of **first applicant**

Title

| | | | | | | | | |

First name(s)

| | | | | | | | | | | | | | | | | | | | |

| | | | | | | | | | | | | | | | | | | | |

Middle name(s)

| | | | | | | | | | | | | | | | | | | | |

| | | | | | | | | | | | | | | | | | | | |

Last name

| | | | | | | | | | | | | | | | | | | | |

| | | | | | | | | | | | | | | | | | | | |

1.2 Is your name different in the will and codicil?

☐ Yes, give the name as it appears in the will or codicil in the box below

| |

☐ No

Note 1.1 –
all correspondence, including the Grant of Representation, will be sent to the first applicant named in this section.

Only list applicants who wish to be named on the grant in this section and they will be required to sign this document. Please note that the names you provide here must match the names provided on your formal ID. E.g. passport or Driving licence.

When there are no executors applying and there are persons aged under 18 benefiting from the estate then two applicants (or at least two) will be needed in Section A. You may wish to contact HMCTS Probate to seek information in regard to who is eligible to apply.

1.3 Your address

Building and street

Second line of address

Town or city

County (optional)

Postcode

1.4 Your home telephone number

1.5 Your mobile/work telephone number

1.6 Your email address

Note 1.6 – we will contact you with any queries via this email address.
We aim to contact you within 10 working days of receipt of your application.

1.7 Title and full name including middle names of **second applicant**

Title

First name(s)

Middle name(s)

Last name

1.8 Is their name different in the will and codicil?

☐ Yes, give the name as it appears in the will or codicil in the box below

☐ No

1.9 Their address

Building and street

Second line of address

Town or city

County (optional)

Postcode

1.10 Their email address

1.11 Title and full name including middle names of **third applicant**

Title

First name(s)

Middle name(s)

Last name

1.12 Is their name different in the will and codicil?

☐ Yes, give the name as it appears in the will or codicil in the box below

☐ No

1.13 Their address

Building and street

Second line of address

Town or city

County (optional)

Postcode

1.14 Their email address

1.15 Title and full name including middle names of **fourth applicant**

Title

First name(s)

Middle name(s)

Last name

1.16 Is their name different in the will and codicil?

☐ Yes, give the name as it appears in the will or codicil in the box below

☐ No

1.17 Their address

Building and street

Second line of address

Town or city

County (optional)

Postcode

1.18 Their email address

SECTION B

The information you provide in this section of the application form will be the basis of your statement of truth, and it will be stored as a public record.

If you need help filling out this form please call the

**Probate Helpline
0300 303 0648**

We cannot provide legal advice

2. About the person who has died

2.1 Forename(s) (including all middle names) as they appear on the Death Certificate

2.2 Surname as it appears on the Death Certificate

2.3 Permanent address

Building and street

Second line of address

Town or city

County (optional)

Postcode

2.4 Date they were born

2.5 Date they died

2.6 Was the person who has died known by any other name in which they held assets?

☐ Yes, **go to question 2.7**

☐ No, **go to question 2.8**

2.7 Please give the details of any other names by which the person who has died held assets.

Full name

Note 2.7 – These names must be ones that will appear on the grant because an asset is in that name. We do not need to know the asset.

2.8 Did the person who died live permanently in England and Wales at the date of death, or intend to return to England and Wales to live permanently? (For legal purposes this generally means they were domiciled in England and Wales. You may wish to seek legal advice about this.)

☐ Yes

☐ No

Note 2.8 – Living permanently means they had either their permanent or principal home in England and Wales at the date of death or they intended to return to England and Wales to live permanently.

2.9 What was the marital status of the person who has died when they died?

☐ Never married

☐ Widowed, their lawful spouse or civil partner having died before them

☐ Married/in a civil partnership - give date

☐ Divorced/civil partnership is dissolved - give date

☐ Judicially separated - give date

2.10 What is the name of the court where the Decree Absolute, Decree of Dissolution of Partnership or Decree of Judicial Separation was issued?

2.11 Did the person who has died own any foreign assets?

☐ Yes, the total value of their foreign assets (not including houses or land)

£

☐ No

Note 2.9 – a civil partnership is a same-sex relationship that has been registered in accordance with the Civil Partnership Act 2004. A marriage is a legal ceremony conducted in UK under the Marriage Acts 1949, 1994 and The Marriage (Same Sex Marriage) Act 2013 or under legislation in any other country by the law applicable there. Date of divorce - this date is on their Decree Absolute, Decree of Dissolution of Partnership or Decree of Judicial Separation. You can get an official copy of these documents from the court that issued them, or from The Divorce Absolute Search Section, Central Family Court, 42–49 High Holborn, London WC1V 6NP.

2.12 Was there any land vested in the person who has died which was settled previously to their death and which remained settled land not withstanding their death?

☐ Yes

☐ No

Only answer this question if no executor to the will is applying

2.13 Was the person who has died or any of their relatives legally adopted in or out of the family?

☐ Yes, **see note 2.13**

☐ No, **go to question 3**

2.14 Please name the legally adopted relatives and give their relationship to the person who has died. Please state whether they were adopted into the family of the person who has died, or 'adopted out' (become part of someone else's family).

Name	Relationship	Adopted **in** or **out**

Note 2.12 – It is rare for estates to be subject to the provisions of the Settled Land Act 1925 but if you know this applies or have any queries please seek legal advice.

Note 2.13 – If you answered Yes to this question we may require additional information to be submitted once we have received your application.

3. The will and any codicils – This section is about the will. You must submit the most recent original will and codicils made since the last will, if there are any.

3.1 What is the date of the will you are submitting to the court?

3.2 Did the person who has died also leave any codicils, made since that will?

☐ Yes, **please provide the original document(s) with your application and list below the dates of the codicils you are submitting to the court.**

☐ No

3.3 Did the person who has died have any wills that were made outside of England and Wales?

☐ Yes

☐ No

3.4 Did the person who has died marry or enter into a Civil Partnership after the date of the will or any codicils?

☐ Yes, please give the date of marriage or civil partnership

☐ No

Only answer this question if no executor to the will is applying

3.5 Is there anyone under 18 years old who receives a gift in the will or a codicil?

☐ Yes, **Please note two applicants will need to apply in Section A. Contact HMCTS Probate to see who is entitled to make the application.**

☐ No

Note 3 – a will does not have to be a formal document. Please make sure you send the original will with your application. If you do not then this will delay your application.

If you have been unable to locate the original will or any codicil and only have a copy and have made all reasonable attempts to locate the original. Please visit GOV. UK (gov.uk/wills-probate-inheritance/if-the-person-left-a-will) to print off the PA13 lost will questionnaire or call 0117 9302430 and quote 'Lost will' and we will supply additional information to help you proceed.

Note 3.2 – a codicil is a document that amends a will.

3.6 Name any executors who are **not** making this application, and explain why.

Reasons for executors not applying:

A – They died before the person who has died.

B – They died after the person who has died (Please include the date they died by their name).

C – Power reserved: they have chosen not to apply, but reserve the right to do so later.

D – Renunciation: they have chosen not to apply, and give up all rights to apply. (Before you send off your application please **read NOTE REASON D**)

E – Power of attorney: they have appointed or wish to appoint another person to act as their attorney to take a Grant of Representation on their behalf (You will also need to complete Section 5 of this application). (Before you send off your application please **read NOTE REASON E**)

F – They lack capacity to act as executor.

Full name(s) of executor(s) **not** applying	A, B, C, D, E or F

Note 3.6 – Executors are the first person who can apply for a grant. We need to know why any executors aren't included in this application. This includes any executors who have pre-deceased. **If you do not provide all of the information this will delay your application.**

Reason C

If any executors are having power reserved, you **must** notify them of the application in writing. The Grant of Representation will only be issued to those people named as applicants in Section A.

Reason D

If you state that an executor has given up their right to apply. We will need to send another form to you to give to the executor, for them to sign. Please visit GOV.UK (gov.uk/wills-probate-inheritance/if-youre-an-executor) to print off the PA15 renunciation form or call 0117 9302430 and quote 'Renunciation' and we will send the renunciation form.

You will need to send the renunciation form to us with this application.

Reason E

If you state that an executor wishes to appoint an attorney or they already have an attorney. We will need to send another form to you to give to the executor for them to sign, or you will need to provide one of the forms mentioned in Section 5.

Please visit GOV.UK (gov.uk/wills-probate-inheritance/if-youre-an-executor) to print off the PA11 attorney form or call 0117 9302430 and quote 'Attorney' and we will send the attorney form.

You will need to send the attorney form to us with this application. The attorney of one executor and an executor acting in their own right may not jointly apply for a Grant of Representation.

Reason F

If you state that an executor lacks capacity and are incapable of managing their property and financial affairs, when we receive this application we may send a medical certificate for the executors' doctor to sign. If you do not already have medical evidence from a qualified practitioner or are using a registered LPA a short form of medical evidence will be required.

Please visit GOV.UK (gov.uk/wills-probate-inheritance/if-youre-an-executor) to print off the PA14 medical certificate or call 0117 9302430 and quote 'Medical evidence' and we will send out the form.

You will need to send the medical certificate to us with this application.

The attorney of one executor and an executor acting in their own right may not jointly apply for a Grant of Representation.

3.7 ☐ The undersigned declare that written notice has been given to all executors who have power reserved to them and are not making this application.

If you fail to give written notice, it is likely to delay your application.

3.8 Did you separate the will for photocopying purposes?

☐ Yes - please explain the details in the box below including who separated it, when they did and why they did it.

☐ No

3.9 Can you confirm the will consisted of the pages now being submitted and no other pages or documents of a testamentary nature or other nature were attached.

☐ Yes

☐ No

4. Relatives of the person who has died

4.1 Did the person who has died leave a surviving spouse or civil partner?

☐ Yes

☐ No

Note 4.1 – 'survive' means that they were alive when the deceased person died.

4.2 How many of the following blood and adoptive relatives did the person who has died have?

Note 4.2 – Please state the **number** of relatives the person who has died had in the relevant sections. If none then put nil or strike through.

		Under 18 years	Over 18 years
a	How many sons or daughters of the person who died survived them?		
b	How many sons or daughters of the person who has died who did not survive them?		
c	How many children of people at 'b' who survived them?		

4.3 Please state the relationship of each of the persons applying for the grant to the person who has died. (If you are applying as an attorney for someone then please state attorney)

Relationship description

First applicant

Second applicant

Third applicant

Fourth applicant

5. Applying as an attorney

5.1 Are you applying as an attorney on behalf of one or more people who are entitled to apply for a Grant of Representation?

☐ Yes, **go to question 5.2**

☐ No, **go to section 6**

5.2 Please give the full names of the person or people on whose behalf you are applying.

```



```

5.3 Please give their address

Building and street

```

```

Second line of address

```

```

Town or city

```

```

County (optional)

```

```

Postcode

```

```

5.4 Is a person on whose behalf you are applying unable to make a decision for themselves due to an impairment of or a disturbance in the functioning of their mind or brain?

☐ Yes, further confirmation of this will be requested by HMCTS Probate.

☐ No

5.5 Has anyone been appointed by the Court of Protection to act on behalf of a person on whose behalf you are applying including the right for a grant of representation?

☐ Yes, **please provide an official copy of the court order with your application**

☐ No

Note 5 – if you are applying on behalf of more than one person, please provide the information requested in this section for the other people you represent on a separate sheet of paper. We will need to send another form to you to give to the executor for them to sign, or you will need to provide one of the forms mentioned in this section.

Please visit GOV.UK (gov.uk/wills-probate-inheritance/if-youre-an-executor) to print off the PA11 attorney form or call 0117 9302430 and quote 'Attorney' and we will send the attorney form.

You will need to send the signed attorney form to us with this application. The attorney of one executor and an executor acting in their own right may not jointly apply for a Grant of Representation.

Where there are persons aged under 18 benefiting from the estate then two applicants (or at least two) will be needed in Section A. You may wish to contact HMCTS Probate to seek information in regard to who is eligible to apply.

Note 5.4 – this applies if they lack capacity under the Mental Capacity Act 2005 and are incapable of managing their property and financial affairs. You may wish to seek legal advice about this.

If you do not already have medical evidence from a qualified practitioner or are using a registered LPA a short form of medical evidence will be required.

Please visit GOV.UK (gov.uk/wills-probate-inheritance/if-youre-an-executor) to print off the PA14 medical certificate or call 0117 9302430 and quote 'medical evidence' and we will send the form.

5.6 Has a person on whose behalf you are applying appointed an attorney under an Enduring Power of Attorney (EPA) or a Property and Financial Affairs Lasting Power of Attorney (LPA)?

☐ Yes, **please provide the original EPA/LPA (or a solicitor's certified copy of it certified on every page.) with your application**

☐ No, **go to Section 6**

5.7 Has the Enduring Power of Attorney (EPA) been registered with the Office of the Public Guardian?

☐ Yes

☐ No

6. Foreign domicile

Note – if you answered Yes, to question 2.8 you don't need to complete this section – please go to Section 7.

6.1 What was the country where the person who died either lived permanently at the date of death or intended to return to live permanently?

6.2 What does the estate in England and Wales of the person has died consist of?

Assets	Values

6.3 Has an entrusting document been issued by the court where the person who has died was domiciled?

☐ Yes, **please provide the official document with your application; if it is not in English, please also provide an official translation. Go to Section 7.**

☐ No

6.4 Has a succession certificate, inheritance certificate or equivalent document been issued by a court or Notary in the country of domicile of the person who has died?

☐ Yes, **please provide the offical document with your application; if it is not in English, please also provide an official translation.**

☐ No

Note 6.3 and 6.4 – these documents may help to support your application. If you do not have any of these documents, you may wish to seek legal advice.

7. Inheritance tax

7.1 Did you complete an IHT400 and IHT421 form?

☐ Yes

☐ No. **Go to question 7.3**

7.2 Provide the numbers from the **IHT421**

Box 3 (gross value) £

Box 5 (net value) £

Go to Legal statement

7.3 Did you complete an **IHT207** form?

☐ Yes

☐ No. **Go to question 7.5**

7.4 Provide the numbers from the **IHT207**

Box A (gross value) £

Box H (net value) £

Go to Legal statement

7.5 Did the deceased die on or after 1 January 2022?

☐ Yes

☐ No. **Go to question 7.9**

7.6 Provide the following values of the estate for inheritance tax

gross value of the estate for inheritance tax £

net value of the estate for inheritance tax £

net qualifying value of the estate £

7.7 Are you claiming against this estate the unused proportion of the inheritance tax nil-rate band of a pre-deceased spouse or civil partner of the deceased?

☐ Yes

☐ No

Note 7 – Before you can apply for a probate grant you need to value the estate of the person who has died. Then you need to pay any Inheritance Tax that is due or be able to show that there is no Inheritance Tax to pay.

Read how to value the estate and report its value to HMRC at https://www.gov.uk/valuing-estate-of-someone-who-died

Note 7.2 – Forms IHT421 and IHT400 must be sent to HMRC only.

After sending them to HMRC wait 20 working days before submitting this probate application.

For details go to www.gov.uk/hmrc/inheritance-tax-account

If the amount in Box 5 is more than £5,000 you will have to pay a probate application fee.

Note 7.4 – Send HMCTS the IHT207 with your probate application. If the amount in Box H is more than £5,000 you will have to pay a probate application fee.

Note 7.5 – If you answered 'Yes' to 2.8 and 'Yes' to 7.5, you are confirming that the estate is an 'excepted estate' and that the person who has died was domiciled in the UK.

Note 7.6 – The gross, net and net qualifying value for IHT will be provided if you used the IHT checker tool accessible at https://www.gov.uk/valuing-estate-of-someone-who-died/estimate-estate-value

Note 7.7 – Only answer this question if the net qualifying value of the estate is between £325,000 and £650,000

7.8 Provide the gross and net value of the estate for probate

gross value of the estate for probate £

net value of the estate for probate £

Go to Legal statement

Note 7.8 – Guidance on how to calculate these values can be found at https://www.gov.uk/applying-for-probate/before-you-apply

7.9 Did you complete the **IHT205** online with HMRC?

☐ Yes, tell us the:

IHT identifier

Gross value £

Net value £

Go to Legal statement

☐ No. **Go to question 7.10**

Note 7.9 – If you reported the estate's value to HMRC online, you do not need to send HMCTS a paper copy of your report

7.10 Provide the numbers from the **IHT205** form.

Box D (gross value) £

Box F (net value) £

Go to Legal statement

Note 7.10 – Send HMCTS the IHT205 with your probate application. Include the IHT217 form if applicable. If the amount in Box F is more than £5,000 you will have to pay a probate application fee.

LEGAL STATEMENT

The undersigned confirms:

- That the last will and any codicils referred to in this application is the last will and testament of the person who has died
- to collect the whole estate
- to keep full details (an inventory) of the estate
- to keep a full account of how the estate has been distributed
- that the estate is an 'excepted estate' and that the person who died was domiciled in the UK (if 'Yes' was given in answer to question 2.8 and question 7.5)

If the Probate Registry (court) asks the undersigned they will:

- Provide the full details of the estate and how it has been distributed
- Return the grant of representation to the court

and understand that:

- The application will be rejected if the information is not provided (if asked)
- Criminal proceedings for fraud may be brought against the undersigned if it is found that the evidence provided is deliberately untruthful or dishonest

The undersigned confirm to administer the estate of the person who has died in accordance to law, and that the application is truthful.

All persons applying for the grant (those listed in Section A) must sign below.

Name of **first applicant**

Signature

Date signed

Name of **second applicant**

Signature

Date signed

Name of **third applicant**

Signature

Date signed

Name of **fourth applicant**

Signature

Date signed

Please send the original form signed by all applicants and required documents with payment to:
HMCTS Probate, PO Box 12625, Harlow, CM20 9QE

Phone 0300 303 0648
Email contactprobate@justice.gov.uk

How are the applicants entitled to apply.

In what capacity are the persons applying entitled to apply?

☐ The executor/s named in the will/codicil of the person who has died

☐ The Attorney/s acting on behalf of the executor/s named in the will/ codicil of the person who has died

☐ Beneficiary/s named in the will/codicil of the person who has died

☐ The Attorney/s acting on behalf of the beneficiary/s named in the will/ codicil of the person who has died

☐ Other (Please state in the box below the reason they are applying)

Equality and diversity questions
(optional)

- **These are optional questions about you**
- **Your answers will not affect your case**
- **We will not share your answers with anyone involved in your case**

Your answers will help us check we are treating people fairly and equally.

These questions should be answered by one executor.

If you are a legal professional completing the form on behalf of an executor don't answer the questions.

How to complete these questions

1. Answer the questions on the next four pages. You can always choose 'prefer not to say' or leave them blank.

2. Send one copy of the completed questionnaire with your application to:

   HMCTS Probate

   PO BOX 12625

   Harlow

   CM20 9QE

Equality and diversity questions

1. What is your main language?

   ☐ English or Welsh, **go to question 3**

   ☐ Other, give details (including British sign language)

   [   ]

   ☐ Prefer not to say, **go to question 3**

2. If you have answered 'Other' in question 1, how well can you speak English?

   ☐ Very well

   ☐ Well

   ☐ Not well

   ☐ Not at all

   ☐ Prefer not to say

3. What is your religion?

   ☐ No religion

   ☐ Christian (all denominations)

   ☐ Buddhist

   ☐ Hindu

   ☐ Jewish

   ☐ Muslim

   ☐ Sikh

   ☐ Any other religion, please describe

   [   ]

   ☐ Prefer not to say

4. What is your date of birth?

   Day   Month   Year
   [   ]   [   ]   [   ]

   ☐ Prefer not to say

5. What is your ethnic group?

☐ Prefer not to say

White

☐ English, Welsh, Scottish, Northern Irish or British

☐ Irish

☐ Gypsy or Irish Traveller

☐ Any other White background, please describe

Mixed/Multiple ethnic groups

☐ White and Black Caribbean

☐ White and Black African

☐ White and Asian

☐ Any other Mixed/Multiple ethnic background, please describe

Asian/Asian British

☐ Indian

☐ Pakistani

☐ Bangladeshi

☐ Chinese

☐ Any other Asian background, please describe

Black/African/Caribbean/Black British

☐ African

☐ Caribbean

☐ Any other Black/African/Caribbean background, please describe

Other ethnic group

☐ Arab

☐ Any other ethnic group, please describe

EQ10 – Equalities questions – Probate (11.20)

6. Do you have any physical or mental health conditions or illnesses lasting or expected to last 12 months or more?

☐ Yes, **go to question 7**

☐ No, **go to question 9**

☐ Prefer not to say, **go to question 9**

7. If Yes, do any of your conditions or illnesses reduce your ability to carry out day-to-day activities?

☐ Yes, a little, **go to question 8**

☐ Yes, a lot, **go to question 8**

☐ Not at all, **go to question 9**

☐ Prefer not to say, **go to question 9**

8. Do any of these conditions or illnesses affect you in any of the following areas?

Tick all options that apply

☐ **Vision** – for example blindness or partial sight

☐ **Hearing** – for example deafness or partial hearing

☐ **Mobility** – for example walking short distances or climbing stairs

☐ **Dexterity** – for example lifting and carrying objects, using a keyboard

☐ **Learning or understanding or concentrating**

☐ **Memory**

☐ **Mental health**

☐ **Stamina or breathing or fatigue**

☐ **Socially or behaviourally** – for example associated with autism, attention deficit disorder or Asperger's syndrome

☐ **Other,** please specify

☐ **None of the above**

EQ10 – Equalities questions – Probate (11.20)

9. Are you currently pregnant or have you been pregnant in
    the last year?

    ☐ Yes

    ☐ No

    ☐ Prefer not to say

10. Which of the following options best describes how you
    think of yourself?

    ☐ Heterosexual or Straight

    ☐ Gay or Lesbian

    ☐ Bisexual

    ☐ Other, please describe

    [   ]

    ☐ Prefer not to say

11. What is your sex?

    ☐ Male

    ☐ Female

    ☐ Prefer not to say

12. Is your gender the same as the sex you were registered at birth?

    ☐ Yes

    ☐ No, my gender is

    [   ]

    ☐ Prefer not to say

13. Are you married or in a legally registered civil partnership?

    ☐ Yes

    ☐ No

    ☐ Prefer not to say

Thank you for answering these questions

Send this questionnaire back with your completed application

Privacy notice

By submitting your answers, you agree that we can collect your information. We'll use it to help us meet our commitment to equality under the Equality Act 2010. You can withdraw your consent or change your answers at any time, see information below in our privacy notice.

For details of the standards we follow when processing your data, please visit the following address https://equality-and-diversity.platform.hmcts.net/privacy-policy

To receive a paper copy of this notice, please call 0300 303 0648

Alternative formats

If you need this form in an alternative format, for example in large print, call 0300 303 0648

EQ10 – Equalities questions – Probate (11.20)

PA15 — **Renunciation** (Will)

This means giving up the right to act as executor/administrator.

Please complete all the boxes then the executor who wishes to renounce should sign in the presence of an independent witness

1. Forename(s) (including all middle names) of the person who has died, as they appear on the Death Certificate

2. Surname of the person who has died, as it appears on the Death Certificate

3. Address

   Building and street

   Second line of address

   Town or city

   County (optional)

   Postcode

4. What was their date of death?

   Day   Month   Year

5. Date of will

   Day   Month   Year

6. Date of codicil

Day

Month

Year

Day

Month

Year

Day

Month

Year

Codicil – This is an addition to the Will that has been signed by the deceased and two witnesses.

7. What is the full name and address of the executor renouncing the will?

Name

Address

Building and street

Second line of address

Town or city

County (optional)

Postcode

Your email address

Residuary legatee and devisee in trust – The person named in the Will who receives the remainder of the estate to hold for the beneficiaries.

8. The executor is

☐ a sole executor and/or residuary legatee and devisee in trust

☐ one of the executors and/or residuary legatee and devisee in trust

9. I the executor named over the page do hereby declare that I have not intermeddled in the estate of the deceased and will not hereafter intermeddle therein with intent to defraud creditors and I do hereby renounce all my right and title to probate and letters of administration with will annexed and execution of the said will (and codicil)

Have not intermeddled in the estate with intent to defraud creditors – Have never been involved in the financial affairs of the deceased since the date of death and will not purposely withhold monies owed by the deceased to others.

Signed as a deed by renouncing executor and/or residuary legatee and devisee in trust

Signature of independent witness

Witnessed by
(print name of witness, this must be an independent person)

Independent Witness – This is someone that is not related to the person renouncing and has no interest in the estate.

Date

Day   Month   Year

Emerald Home Lawyer Guide

A Practical Guide to Residential Conveyancing

A Comprehensive Guide to Conveyancing Registered Land.

The book covers the following areas:

- Conveyancing of registered land
- Acting for the seller
- Law Society's formulae for exchanging of contracts
- Acting for the purchaser in freehold and leasehold matters
- Preparing for completion
- Completing a transaction
- Registering at the Land Registry
- Post completion work

Peter Wade

An Emerald guide to

Powers of Attorney

The Complete Guide to All Aspects of Creating A Power of Attorney

The book covers the following areas in detail:

- Lasting Power of Attorney
- Enduring Power of Attorney
- Ordinary Powers of Attorney
- Donors Capacity
- Risk of Abuse
- Certificate Providers
- Registering the Lasting Power of Attorney
- Duties and Responsibilities of Attorneys
- Property and Financial Affairs – Lasting Powers of Attorney
- Health & Welfare – Lasting Powers of Attorney

Peter Wade